HIP-HOP STARS

EMINEM

HIP-HOP STARS

Beastie Boys
Sean Combs
Missy Elliott
Eminem
Jay-Z

LL Cool J
Queen Latifah
Run–DMC
Tupac Shakur
Russell Simmons

HIP-HOP STARS

EMINEM

Dennis Abrams

CHELSEA HOUSE
PUBLISHERS
An imprint of Infobase Publishing

EMINEM

Chelsea House
An imprint of Infobase Publishing
132 West 31st Street
New York, NY 10001

Library of Congress Cataloging-in-Publication Data

Abrams, Dennis, 1960-
    Eminem / Dennis Abrams.
        p. cm. — (Hip-hop stars)
    Includes bibliographical references (p. 85) and index.
    ISBN-13: 978-0-7910-9479-2 (hardcover)
    ISBN-10: 0-7910-9479-0 (hardcover)

    1. Eminem (Musician)—Juvenile literature. 2. Rap musicians—United States—Biography—Juvenile literature. I. Title. II. Series.

    ML3930.E46A27 2007
    782.421649092—dc22   2007001327

Chelsea House books are available at special discounts when purchased in bulk quantities for businesses, associations, institutions, or sales promotions. Please call our Special Sales Department in New York at (212) 967-8800 or (800) 322-8755.

You can find Chelsea House on the World Wide Web at http://www.chelseahouse.com

Text design by Erik Lindstrom
Cover design by Ben Peterson

Printed in the United States of America

Bang FOF 10 9 8 7 6 5 4 3 2 1

This book is printed on acid-free paper.

All links and Web addresses were checked and verified to be correct at the time of publication. Because of the dynamic nature of the Web, some addresses and links may have changed since publication and may no longer be valid.

CONTENTS

Hip-Hop: A Brief History by Chuck D 6

1 Who Is He? 11

2 Childhood 20

3 Rock Bottom 28

4 The Birth of Slim Shady 41

5 I'm Just Marshall Mathers 56

6 The Eminem Show 70

7 Just Lose It 79

8 The End of Slim Shady? 85

Discography 90

Chronology 91

Glossary 94

Bibliography 95

Further Reading 97

Index 99

Hip-Hop: A Brief History

Like the air we breathe, hip-hop seems to be everywhere. The lifestyle that many thought would be a passing fad has, three decades later, grown to become a permanent part of world culture. Hip-hop artists have become some of today's heroes, replacing the comic book worship of decades past and joining athletes and movie stars as the people kids dream of being. Names like 50 Cent, P. Diddy, Russell Simmons, Jay-Z, Foxy Brown, Snoop Dogg, and Flavor Flav now ring as familiar as Elvis, Babe Ruth, Marilyn Monroe, and Charlie Chaplin.

While the general public knows many of the names, videos, and songs branded by the big companies that make them popular, it's also important to know the holy trinity, the founding fathers of hip-hop: Kool DJ Herc, Grandmaster

Flash, and Afrika Bambaataa. All are deejays who played and presented the records that rappers and dancers delighted themselves upon. Bambaataa single-handedly stopped the gang wars in the 1970s with the themes of peace, unity, love and having fun.

Hip-hop is simply a term for a form of artistic creativity that spawned from New York City—more precisely the Bronx—in the early to mid 1970s. Amidst the urban decay in the areas where black and Hispanic people dwelled, economic, educational and environmental resources were depleted. Jobs and businesses were all but moved away. Living conditions were of a lower standard than the rest of the city and country. Last but not least, art and sports programs in the schools were the first to be cut for the sake of lowering budgets; thus, music classes, teaching the subject's history and techniques, were all but lost.

From these ashes, like a phoenix, rose an art form. Through the love of technology and records found in family collections or even those tossed out on the street, the deejay emerged. Different from the ones heard on the radio, these folk were innovating a style that was popular on the island of Jamaica. Two turntables kept the music continuous, with the occasional voice on top of the records. This was the very humble beginning of rap music.

Rap music is actually two distinct words: rap and music. "Rap" is the vocal application that is used on top of the music. On a vocal spectrum, it is between talking and singing and is one of the few alternatives for vocalizing to emerge in the last 50 years. It's important to know that inventors and artists are side by side in the importance of music's development. Let's remember that inventor Thomas A. Edison created the first recording, with "Mary Had a Little Lamb" in 1878, most likely in New Jersey, the same state where the first rap recording—Sugarhill Gang's "Rappers Delight"—was made almost 100 years later, in 1979.

It's hard to separate the importance of history, science, language arts, and education when discussing music. Because of the social silencing of black people in the United States from slavery in the 1600s to civil rights in the 1960s, much sentiment, dialogue, and soul is wrapped within their cultural expression of music. In eighteenth-century New Orleans, slaves gathered on Sundays in Congo Square to socialize and play music. Within this captivity many dialects, customs, and styles combined with instrumentation, vocals, and rhythm to form a musical signal or code of preservation. These are the foundations of jazz and the blues. Likewise, it's impossible to separate hip-hop and rap music from the creativity of the past. Look within the expression and words of black music and you'll get a reflection of history itself. The four creative elements of hip-hop—emceeing (the art of vocalization); deejaying (the musician-like manipulation of records); break dancing (the body expression of the music); and graffiti (the drawn graphic expression of the culture)—have been intertwined in the community before and since slavery.

However, just because these expressions were introduced by the black–Hispanic underclass, doesn't mean that others cannot create or appreciate hip-hop. Hip-hop is a cultural language used best to unite the human family all around the world. To peep the global explosion, one need not search far. Starting just north of the U.S. border, Canadian hip-hop has featured indigenous rappers who are infusing different language and dialect flows into their work, from Alaskan Eskimo to French flowing cats from Montreal and the rest of the Quebec's provincial region. Few know that France for many years has been the second largest hip-hop nation, measured not just by high sales numbers, but also by a very political philosophy. Hip-hop has been alive and present since the mid-1980s in Japan and other Asian countries. Australia has been a hotbed in welcoming world rap acts, and it has also created its own vibrant hip-hop scene, with the reminder of its government's takeover of indigenous people reflected in every rapper's flow and rhyme. As a rhythm of the people, the continents of Africa and South America (especially Ghana, Senegal, and South Africa, Brazil, Surinam, and Argentina) have long mixed traditional homage into the new beats and rhyme of this millennium.

Hip-hop has been used to help Brazilian kids learn English when school systems failed to bridge the difficult language gap of Portuguese and patois to American English. It has entertained and enlightened youth, and has engaged political discussion in society, continuing the tradition of the African griots (storytellers) and folk singers.

For the past 25 years, hip-hop has been bought, sold, followed, loved, hated, praised, and blamed. History has shown that other cultural music forms in the United States have been just as misunderstood and held under public scrutiny. The history of the people who originated the art form can be found in the music itself. The timeline of recorded rap music spans more than a quarter century, and that is history in itself.

Presidents, kings, queens, fame, famine, infamy, from the great wall of China to the Berlin wall, food, drugs, cars, hate, and love have been rhymed and scratched. This gives plenty reason for social study. And I don't know what can be more fun than learning the history of something so relevant to young minds and souls, as music.

Who Is He?

He was born Marshall Bruce Mathers III. He is best known to the public by his stage name, Eminem. In many of his songs and videos, he plays the role of Slim Shady. The combination has been powerful and successful. The mix of Marshall Mathers the man, Eminem the rapper, and Slim Shady the evil alter ego, has captivated and intrigued audiences worldwide.

Eminem is one of the world's most popular rap artists. Between 1999 and 2006, he sold more than 73,000,000 albums worldwide. He is one of the top-selling rappers of all time, second only to the late Tupac Shakur. (Interestingly, Eminem produced Tupac's album *Loyal to the Game*. It is the eighth album of remixes and previously unreleased material to be released since Tupac's murder in 1996.)

Controversy has not hindered the success of notorious rapper Eminem. With countless honors and awards, including nine Grammy's, nine MTV Video Music Awards, and an Academy Award, Eminem remains one of today's most successful rappers. Known for deftly mixing smart humor with controversial and offensive language, Eminem continues to both offend and affect his listeners.

Although he is an artist who does not stick to the tried-and-true methods but rather strikes out on his own into wildly original territory, Eminem has been able to achieve both popular acclaim and critical success. His broad appeal is undeniable, and his popularity with his fans is matched only by the praise he has received from critics and fellow musicians. Eminem has won nine Grammy Awards, which are considered the music industry's highest honor, and nine MTV Video Awards. He has even won an Academy Award.

IMPORTANCE AS A HIP-HOP ARTIST

Eminem's importance as a hip-hop artist cannot be overstated. To many critics, he is as important to rap music as Elvis Presley was to rock and roll.

Elvis Presley burst into America's consciousness in 1956 with his first big hit, "Heartbreak Hotel." In it he combined several different kinds of traditional American music. He combined rhythm and blues (R&B) music, which was traditionally enjoyed by blacks, with country and western music, which was traditionally listened to by whites. What emerged from the mix was rock and roll. This new music appealed to both fans of R&B and fans of country. By blending different types of music, Elvis helped break down music's cultural boundaries.

Spin magazine editor Alan Light compared this fusion to Eminem's own blending of styles, as quoted in Chuck Weiner's *Eminem Talking*:

> Eminem is very true to hip-hop but does bring some more rock and roll sensibility to it. It's not about him copying, it's not about imitation. It's about being inside of that enough to really incorporate it and do something different. And I think that's why people respond to it.

The two musicians also share a similar background: Elvis grew up poor, listening to rhythm and blues music. Eminem

In the song "Without Me" Eminem says "Though I'm not the first king of controversy/I am the worst thing since Elvis Presley, to do Black Music so selfishly." Since first breaking into the music scene in 1999, Eminem has been compared to Elvis Presley for achieving success in a traditionally black music genre. In the 1950's Elvis Presley prevailed as the "King of Rock 'n' Roll," opening this music genre to both blacks and whites.

grew up poor, listening to rap or hip-hop, known at the time as music for black urban youth. Like Elvis, he creates music that respects musical traditions, and brings different audiences together through music. Also like Elvis, Eminem has been accused of "using" or exploiting black music to get rich. As Eminem jokingly raps in "Without Me" from the CD *The Eminem Show*, "Though I'm not the first king of controversy/I am the worst thing since Elvis Presley, to do Black Music so selfishly/and use it to get myself wealthy."

Eminem has created hip-hop that transcends, or goes beyond, the lines that divide black and white music. Fans of hip-hop admire him for his strong lyrical talents. He is praised for his ability to change his flow and style within a song without losing a beat. His rhyme sense, use of language, and humor all make him preeminent among today's hip-hop artists. A track by Eminem stands out. He sounds like nobody else.

It is more than his rap style that sets him apart from other rappers. His choice of subject matter helps to distinguish him. Before Eminem came on the scene, gangsta rap was the dominant style of rap. When it first emerged in the early 1980s, gangsta rap covered topics like alienation, drugs, and being poor. Rappers spoke to their audience about the struggle against police and other authority figures. After the violent deaths of Tupac Shakur and the Notorious B.I.G., however, the music changed. Suddenly, the violence in gangsta rap lyrics felt a little too "real." In addition, as the rappers became successful, they moved away from the lifestyle that generated their lyrics in the first place. Gangsta rap moved from songs about life on the streets to music about life at the top. Songs about "bling," women, and the power of money to buy anything ruled the charts. The music moved from documenting the struggles of the poor to celebrating the joys of being rich. Lyrics glorified a life of conspicuous consumption, a life of wearing clothes by Prada and guzzling Kristal champagne.

Eminem's music and life reject the glorification of money and its rewards. Writing largely about his own experiences, Eminem is able to discuss topics that many people can relate to. He writes about drug abuse. He writes about his mother

ELVIS

The importance of Elvis Presley in American culture cannot be underestimated. Born January 8, 1935, in Tupelo, Mississippi, Elvis Aaron Presley's humble beginnings in no way indicated the impact he would have on the world. Growing up in the American south and heavily influenced by its varied musical cultures, Elvis brought a new sound to the mainstream public. He started as a singer of rockabilly. But borrowing songs from rhythm and blues (R&B) as well as country, he helped create rock and roll.

He also helped bridge the gap between white and black culture in the United States. Even during the 1950s, Elvis publicly acknowledged his debt to black musicians. Musicians such as B.B. King, Jackie Wilson, and Fats Domino had a huge influence on his music.

Many have accused Elvis of "stealing" black music to make money. It is more likely that the blending of different sounds in his music, combined with his huge popularity, helped erase the differences between black and white music. This allowed many black artists to reach audiences they had never been able to reach before.

As rock and roll legend Little Richard said to Graceland's National Historic Landmark Nomination reports, "He was an integrator. Elvis was a blessing. They wouldn't let black music through. He opened the door for black music."

Elvis also became a movie star, appearing in 33 films, along with several television specials and countless successful live concerts. Still tremendously popular, he has sold more records than any other artist. Plagued by an excessive lifestyle, Elvis died at Graceland, his famous estate, on August 16, 1977.

and his troubled childhood. He writes about his ongoing relationship with his ex-wife Kim Mathers. He writes about growing up poor in Detroit. He writes about being white and living in a black neighborhood. He writes about his love for his daughter, Hailie.

Writing about these things brings rap back to its roots. Eminem raps realistically and honestly about his own life. By doing so, he is respected within the black community like no other white rapper before him. Whereas Vanilla Ice, a successful white rapper from the 1980s who tried to change the face of hip-hop, only *pretended* to be an authentic street-smart rapper, Eminem *is* a rapper, from the bottom of his soul. As Missy Elliot said in *Eminem Talking*, "I love him 'cos he's white and he knows he's white. He's just him and whatever he raps about is what he's going through. I ain't mad at that." Eminem's authenticity transcends skin color, but his being white allows him to appeal to a large white audience as well. It's this ability to bring together black and white fans that has made him so hugely successful. For his audience, he goes beyond the labels of "black" or "white." He's simply Eminem.

By writing about his own life and feelings, Eminem is able to make his fans think about their own lives. For example, by expressing his anger and feelings about his mother and his childhood, he allows his listeners to consider their own childhoods. Using his music to release his inner demons, he allows his listeners to release theirs.

CONTROVERSIAL

Eminem's music is not without controversy. His detractors accuse him of being misogynistic (disliking women). He has been accused of being homophobic (disliking gay people). Many people feel that, because his lyrics show disdain for women and gays, he is encouraging his fans to feel the same hatred toward these groups.

Eminem claims that his lyrics are not always meant to be taken seriously. He says that his character Slim Shady (as first

Eminem created his alter ego, Slim Shady, when he was a member of the rap group D12. Slim Shady is a character used to express anger and rage Eminem felt but never acted on. Eminem claims that Slim Shady is the darker, more evil side of his personality.

unveiled in the song "My Name Is . . .") is just that, a character. Slim Shady, Eminem says, does not necessarily represent what Eminem truly feels. However, many of his fans take everything he says literally; they do not understand when he is being serious and when he is joking.

What some of his younger fans may not understand is that Eminem uses the character of Slim Shady to address taboos—the thoughts that people may have, but are ashamed to admit. Although they are not "politically correct," he feels that it's important to joke about these feelings, to bring them out into the open. By doing that, people will realize how ridiculous they can be.

As Eminem has said, according to *Eminem Talking*, "Slim Shady is just the evil thoughts that come into my head. Things I shouldn't be thinking about. Not to be gimmicky, but people should be able to determine when I'm serious and when I'm [joking] around. That's why a lot of my songs are funny. I got a warped sense of humor, I guess."

Many of his critics have accused him of having anger-management issues. Many of his lyrics express an impulsive anger that he felt while writing the song, but that he no longer has. In songs like "'97 Bonnie and Clyde" and "Kim," he expresses violent thoughts and fantasies about his ex-wife, Kim. Did he literally want to murder his wife as he does in the song? Probably not. By writing down and rapping about his feelings, he is able to release them. As a performer, he shares his feelings with the world.

Where did Eminem's anger come from? How did his upbringing make him the hip-hop artist that he has become? These are complicated questions. Marshall Mathers became the performer Eminem. Eminem uses the character Slim Shady to express the anger, humor, and rage that Marshall Mathers feels about the world.

How did Marshall Mathers become Eminem and Slim Shady? Who is the real Marshall Mathers?

Childhood

The year was 1970. Fifteen-year-old Debbie Nelson was a back-up singer in a band. The band was called Daddy Warbucks. Despite a seven-year age difference, Debbie fell in love with the band's drummer, Marshall Mathers Jr. The two soon married, and on October 17, 1972, Marshall Mathers III, the future Eminem, was born in the town of St. Joseph, near Kansas City, Missouri.

According to Debbie, after giving birth she suffered from toxemia poisoning (also known as blood poisoning) and went into a coma. While she was sick, her husband took the opportunity to name his son after himself. The gifts of life and a name were just about all Marshall Mathers Jr. ever gave his son. Although nearly a child herself, Debbie was thrilled to have a son. Her husband had doubts about being tied down. Marshall Mathers Jr. soon abandoned his family, although there is some question as to when it happened. In any case, Eminem has had no contact with his father. (When Eminem was in his teens, he wrote several letters to his father in California. According to Debbie, they all came back marked "return to sender.")

Debbie loved her son and tried to do her best for him. But by all reports, being a mother was not easy for her. The family was very poor. Because of this, Debbie and Marshall moved frequently. Sometimes they lived in public housing, sometimes in a trailer park. They even lived with other relatives, including Eminem's great-aunt Edna. He mentions her in his song "Evil Deeds" on the CD *Encore*.

Debbie Mathers suffered from severe mood swings. Sometimes she was a loving, affectionate, and doting mother. At other times, she became quiet and withdrawn, and she was unable to care for her son or herself. Sometimes she would get extraordinarily angry for no apparent reason. During those periods, she would yell and scream at her son. She would blame him for everything that was wrong in her life.

It has also been suggested that Debbie Mathers suffered from a mental illness called Munchausen syndrome by proxy. Munchausen syndrome by proxy affects the caregiver of a child, usually the mother, who either pretends the child is sick, or, in some cases, actually causes illnesses or harms the child. She does this to gain attention and sympathy for herself in her role as "worried" and "loving" parent. Technically, Munchausen syndrome by proxy is considered a form of child abuse.

In 1996, a social worker raised the possibility of Munchausen syndrome by proxy during an investigation of Debbie's mistreatment of her second child, Nathan Samra-Mathers. Eminem also accused his mother of having this illness in the song *Cleaning Out My Closet* on the CD *The Eminem Show*, "My whole life I

Eminem has blamed the painful childhood described in many of his songs on his mother, Debbie Mathers-Briggs *(above)*. In interviews and songs, he has accused his mother of abusing drugs, experiencing extreme mood swings, and even suffering from Munchausen syndrome by proxy. Mathers-Brigg has publicly denied most of her son's accusations.

was made to believe I was sick when I wasn't . . . it makes you sick to ya stomach/doesn't it?"

Debbie's drug use added to her instability. She legally took the prescription drugs Vicodin and Valium. In numerous interviews and songs, Eminem accused his mother of abusing these drugs. Debbie Mathers denied the accusations. She eventually sued her son in court on charges of defamation of character.

It is important to note that Debbie Mathers denies most of Eminem's claims about his childhood. She says that she was a good mother. She says that it was because of her love and support that Marshall was able to survive and succeed.

Given his turbulent relationship with his mother, it is not surprising that some of the happiest times of Marshall's early childhood were when he lived with other relatives. He became extremely close to his mother's younger brother, Ronnie Polkinghorn. Technically Marshall was Ronnie's nephew. But since Ronnie was only four months older than his nephew, he became Eminem's best friend and constant source of support. The two were inseparable.

In 1980, when Marshall was just eight years old, he and Debbie moved from Missouri to Warren, in East Detroit, Michigan. Marshall was miserable. He missed Ronnie and hated Detroit. His behavior changed. In Missouri, he had been an outgoing and happy child. After the move, living in Detroit, he became quiet and withdrawn.

LIVING IN DETROIT

Life in Detroit was difficult for Marshall. His mother struggled to make ends meet. Because they often couldn't pay the rent, they frequently moved from one house to another and Marshall constantly had to change schools.

The house where they lived a majority of the time had been in Debbie's family for years and was located on 8 Mile Road. 8 Mile Road is a major dividing line in Detroit. On the city side of the road (where the family's house was) the population is mostly black. The Mathers were one of only three white families on their block. The other side of 8 Mile Road is considered the suburbs. There, the population is mostly white.

8 Mile Road is a physical and cultural dividing line separating the predominately white suburbs from the predominantly black urban area in Detroit, Michigan. Marshall Mathers lived for a majority of his life on 8 Mile Road, one of the only white people in a largely black neighborhood that had high rates of unemployment, poverty, and drug use.

The blocks surrounding 8 Mile Road made up a tough neighborhood to live in. Although divided into black and white areas, they had a lot in common. Unemployment was high. Poverty and drugs took their toll. A sense of hopelessness prevailed. Violence was a way of life.

Young Marshall was poor, small for his age, and skinny. He was also a white male in a predominantly black neighborhood. Because of all those factors, he was a prime target for bullies. His

DETROIT

Detroit is the largest city in Michigan. In 1701, French fur traders founded the city along the Detroit River. Today, it is known as a center of automotive manufacturing and a major source of popular music. Both of these legacies are honored by the city's two nick-names—Motor City and Motown.

In 2005, Detroit was the United States' eleventh-most-popu-lated city, with 886,675 residents. However, this is less than half the population the city had at its peak in 1950. Since that year, the city has been in a state of decline.

Several factors have contributed to this state of affairs: The auto industry has faced challenges from foreign automakers, which has led to a loss of jobs. Racial tensions between blacks and whites exploded in major riots in 1967. These riots, com-bined with court-ordered busing, caused many white residents to leave the city. Those left behind in Detroit tended to be black and poor.

They faced a city where large numbers of buildings and homes had been abandoned. In the 1970s and 1980s heroin and crack cocaine hit the streets of most big cities in the United States, including Detroit. Drug-related crimes and violence among competing drug dealers rose. This was the city that Marshall Mathers grew up in.

Recently the city has shown new signs of life. Casinos have been built. The Detroit Tigers have moved into a new home, Comerica Park. The Detroit Lions have returned to Detroit from years of playing in Pontiac. New office buildings have been built, hotels have been redeveloped, and the first portions of the Detroit River Walk have been laid down. With these improve-ments, and more to come, it is hoped that the city's worst days are behind it.

Eminem was born Marshall Bruce Mathers III on October 17, 1972. Abandoned by his father, he was raised by his mother, Debbie Mathers. Eminem had an extremely poor upbringing, at times living in public housing and trailer parks. Photographed above is the entrance to Chateau Clinton, a mobile home park where Eminem lived in Sterling Heights, Michigan.

life in Detroit was miserable. He would be teased and physically attacked on his way to school, at school, and on his way home from school. For Marshall, there was no escape.

Because of the constant torment, he began to hate school. Although obviously bright, he did poorly in class. He often pretended to be sick to avoid going to school. Things came to a head in 1982. According to Marshall, he had spent that year in junior high being tormented by one particular student named D'Angelo Bailey. D'Angelo had attacked Marshall on several occasions, but the events of January 13 proved to be nearly fatal. On that date, during recess, Marshall was hit in the head by a snowball containing a rock or some other heavy object. He was then slammed headfirst into the asphalt and kicked repeatedly in the head. Eminem claims that D'Angelo did this. D'Angelo was known to be the biggest kid in school. Marshall was the smallest.

Marshall was severely wounded in the attack. Dazed and confused by the repeated blows to the head, he was sent home for the day. Upon arriving home, he began bleeding from his ears. He was then rushed to the hospital. He went into a coma for ten days. According to his doctors, he nearly died. Fortunately, he came through without any major long-term damage.

This incident became the basis for the song "Brain Damage" from the CD *The Slim Shady Show*. As Eminem says in the lyrics, "I was harassed daily by this fat kid named D'Angelo Bailey/An eighth-grader who acted obnoxious, 'cause his father boxes/So every day he'd shove me in the lockers." D'Angelo Bailey sued Marshall about the song, accusing him of libel and infringing on his privacy. The suit was dismissed. Today, Bailey occasionally signs autographs for curious Eminem fans.

Debbie Mathers had had enough of living in Detroit. Soon after the attack and Marshall's recovery, Debbie and her son moved back to Kansas City. There, Marshall would be reunited with his beloved Uncle Ronnie. Ronnie would introduce Marshall to his favorite new music—hip-hop.

Rock Bottom

The roots of hip-hop music are in West African and African American music. Arguably, one could trace the music back to the griots of West Africa. A griot is a West African storyteller who recites poems and tales that tell the history of his family, village, and tribe. He accompanies his recitation on a stringed instrument.

Hip-hop as we know it began at block parties in New York City. Popular music like soul, disco, and funk was often played at the parties. There, DJs such as Grandmaster Flash and Kool DJ Herc began isolating the percussion breaks in the records (the most danceable parts) and extending them. They did this using an audio mixer and two records.

This use of extended percussion breaks led to the development of mixing and scratching techniques. Scratching was invented by Grandwizard Theodore in 1977 and was used in DJ records such as Grandmaster Flash's "Adventures on the Wheels of Steel." "Scratching" is created by moving a vinyl record back and forth while it's being played on the turntable. It is one of the most distinctive sounds of hip-hop.

As hip-hop grew in popularity, performers began speaking while the music played. These performers became known as MCs, or emcees. They often performed for hours at a time. They began improvising on a simple four-count beat with a basic chorus. Gradually, the MCs expanded their approach to rap. They became more varied in their vocals and rhythms. The development of scratching led to the popularization of remixes.

With that, hip-hop moved from live music at parties to commercial recordings. "King Tim III (Personality Jock)" by the Fatback Band is generally considered to be the first recorded hip-hop song, but it was "Rapper's Delight" by the Sugarhill Gang that was the first to win mainstream popularity. "Rapper's Delight" even became a Top 40 hit on the U.S. Billboard pop singles chart. Other hit songs such as "The Breaks" by Kurtis Blow and "Freedom" by Grandmaster Flash and the Furious Five achieved popularity as well. Hip-hop soon became trendy.

Performers like Kurtis Blow starred in TV commercials. Break dancing, a street dance style that originated in the South Bronx, began to enter the mainstream. With that, Hollywood took notice. In 1983, *Breakin'*, the first movie about hip-hop and break dancing, was released. The movie was inspired by a German documentary set in the Los Angeles multiracial hip-hop club Radiotron. *Breakin'* had a standard musical plot about a struggling jazz dancer who meets two break-dancers. She learns to love the new dance style. Against all the odds, she becomes a star dancer on the streets of Los Angeles.

In the early 1980's, rap music was starting to become popular with a mainstream audience. Performers such as Kurtis Blow *(above)* and LL Cool J were breakthrough artists who influenced Eminem when he was just a kid, learning about rap music from his Uncle Ronnie.

A WHOLE NEW WORLD

Breakin' featured many early hip-hop dancers and musicians. It included dancer Boogaloo Shrimp and, in his movie debut as a club MC, Ice-T. The soundtrack to the movie would open Marshall Mathers's ears to a whole new world. After listening to it, his life would never be the same. According to *Eminem Talking*, Eminem said, "When I was nine years old, my Uncle Ronnie put me on to the *Breakin'* soundtrack. The first rap song I ever heard was Ice-T, 'Reckless.' From LL [Cool J] to the Fat Boys, and all that [stuff] I was fascinated. When LL first came out with 'I'm Bad' I wanted to do it, to rhyme. Standing in front of the mirror, I wanted to be like LL."

Eminem's Uncle Ronnie was a huge fan of rap. He was a rapper himself, and he made tapes for Marshall, who played them constantly. For the next couple of years, Marshall listened to and studied rap music, but he wasn't ready to begin performing. He was impressed and intimidated by Ronnie's talents as a rapper. He felt too shy and self-conscious to let Ronnie know that he also wanted to be a rapper.

Things were going well for Marshall. He was happy spending his time with Ronnie. He'd discovered and fallen in love with hip-hop. His mother, Debbie, was also doing well. She was more stable then she'd been in years. In 1986, she had a second child, Marshall's half brother, Nathan, nicknamed "Nate." The next year, though, Debbie decided to move the family back to Detroit, this time for good. Marshall was devastated. He had bad memories of life in Detroit. He couldn't stand the thought of being separated from Ronnie for a second time. Once again, after the move, Marshall went through a period of severe depression.

EARLY RAPPING

This time his depression lifted relatively quickly. Older now, he found rap music provided a way to escape during times of sadness and trouble. The musical energy and verbal rhythms clicked with something deep inside Marshall. They provided interests outside of himself and his own troubles.

He listened to everyone. Tupac Shakur, Run DMC, NWA, and Big Daddy Kane were among his favorites. One of the

BREAK DANCING

Break dancing (also known as breaking or b-boying) is a street dance style. It evolved as part of the hip-hop movement in the South Bronx section of New York City during the 1970s.

No one can say with certainty how it began. Many think that break dancing began as a method for rival street gangs to settle disputes without fighting. Whichever dancer (or dancers) had the most complicated and innovative moves won the fight.

The dance style itself is a mixture of aerobic styles. It includes forms, motions, and maneuvers used in martial arts (especially Brazilian capoeira), gymnastics, and popular funk dance. The term "break" comes from the quick and energetic break in the song during which dancers showed off their best moves.

Break dancing quickly became a pop-culture phenomenon. It received massive media attention. Break-dancers appeared on television and in movies and music videos. Movies such as *Flashdance, Wild Style, Beat Street, Breakin'*, and *Breakin' 2: Electric Boogaloo* brought break-dance culture worldwide.

Its impact has been huge. The popularity of break dancing helped bring hip-hop music into the mainstream, and its impact on fashion can still be seen today. Flat-soled sneakers, track-suits, and hooded nylon jackets were essential to b-boys in the 1980s. Although b-boys of today dress differently than those of the 1980s, one thing remains constant—dressing "fresh."

groups that had the biggest influence on Marshall was the Beastie Boys. Coming out of New York City, the Beastie Boys was the first important white rap group. Hearing white rappers opened up new possibilities for Marshall. As he said in *Eminem Talking*,

> When I first heard the Beasties, I didn't know they were white. I just thought it was the craziest [stuff] I had ever heard. I was probably 12. Then I saw the video and saw that they were white, and I went, "Wow." I thought, "Hey, I can do this." The Beastie Boys were what really did for me. I was like, "This [stuff] is so dope!" That's when I decided to rap.

Marshall began taking rap seriously. He would make beat tapes just like his Uncle Ronnie and rhyme to them. He began to focus more and more on his lyrics. He worked hard on making them faster and more focused. He worked on getting his vocal rhythms down. He became so focused on rapping that he even read dictionaries late into the night, trying to build his vocabulary to make his raps more interesting.

With his new friend MC Proof, he began sneaking into Osborn High School at lunchtime. There, he would participate in "battle rapping" in the cafeteria or on the playground. Battle rapping is a head-to-head competition between two rappers. The two rappers trade off rhymes, and the first to break the flow is the loser of the battle. MC Proof recalled to *Rolling Stone*, "It was a little like [the movie] *White Men Can't Jump*. Everybody thought [because he was white] that he'd be easy to beat, and they got smoked every time."

For the first time in his life, Marshall was able to win the respect of his peers. This public acknowledgment of his skills did a great deal for his self-esteem. He'd found something that he was better at than anyone else he knew. He was so good that before long no student at the school would take him on. Marshall knew that rap was definitely a viable path for his

In this 1987 photograph, the Beastie Boys are pictured with rap music pioneers, Run-DMC. Eminem has said that the Beastie Boys greatly influenced his rap career. When he first learned that the Beastie Boys were three white kids performing rap music, he started to believe in the possibility of becoming a rapper.

future. But he'd have to move on from battle rapping at school to hone his skills.

He also needed a new name. He chose "Eminem" as his stage name. The name "Eminem" came from his initials, "M" and "M." Marshall liked the new name because it was derived from his own, yet it was still different.

Not only was he gaining confidence as a rapper, but also his personal life was going well. He met the girl who would become his high school sweetheart, the mother of his child, and his wife. Her name was Kimberly Ann Scott. Marshall and Kim met at the house of one of his friends. She came over and introduced herself while he was lip-synching to LL Cool J songs and jumping on the furniture. When they met he was 15 and she was just 13.

For Marshall, attending school was not a high priority. Hip-hop was all that mattered to him. He skipped school more often than he was there. Ultimately, when he was 17, he dropped out of high school. After failing ninth grade for the third time, he had had enough.

Marshall's mom insisted that he help bring money into the household. He begrudgingly worked a series of meaningless jobs. He worked at a factory called Gibbs Machinery. He swept floors. He worked at Little Caesar's Pizza. But no matter how hard he worked there was always time for rap. Every spare moment was devoted to improving his craft as a rapper.

It took a long while for Eminem to establish himself as a presence in the music scene. He had grown up with mostly black friends and was comfortable with blacks. But at first, black audiences were uncomfortable with him. For them, hip-hop was music performed by blacks for predominantly black audiences. Early white rappers such as Marky Mark and the Funky Bunch and Vanilla Ice had little or no credibility within the black community. Their appeal was strictly to white audiences who wanted to sample rap without listening to anything hardcore. They gave white rappers a bad name.

Eminem had his work cut out for him. First, there were the difficulties that anyone faces trying to break into show business. Only a few people who try ultimately succeed. Also, he would have to overcome the stigma of being a white rapper. He would have to work twice as hard as any black rapper to prove himself to a black audience.

As Eminem remembered in *Eminem Talking,*

I was booed off stage in the early days, but I just didn't [care]. I started going around Detroit with MCs and winning rap competitions. I was like "You may as well give me my respect, because I'll take it either way" . . . Was it hard to win respect from the homies? Sure, I had to work hard to prove myself—a lot harder than the average rapper who's black. But that's only natural; rap is a predominantly black music. If I'm coming into this game, I've got to work harder if I don't want to get looked at as a joke.

There was one more obstacle in Eminem's path: gaining his Uncle Ronnie's support. Ronnie had come to Detroit for a long visit. Marshall was thrilled to have him around. He took the opportunity to share with his uncle his dream of becoming a rap star.

Marshall was shocked at his uncle's response. Ronnie told his nephew that he had given up on rap. He told Marshall that his dreams were unrealistic and that he'd never be able to achieve his goals. Marshall was saddened by Ronnie's negative attitude, but it left him even more driven to make his dreams a reality. Unlike his uncle, he was determined never to give up hope.

He began getting his first breaks. Based on tapes he'd made, he was invited to perform at the Saturday night open mic nights at the Hip-Hop Club. Located at West 7 Mile, the Hip-Hop Club was at the center of Detroit's hip-hop scene. If Eminem could prove himself there, it would be a major step forward in his career.

His first night there was a disaster. The crowd started booing the moment he walked on the stage. They booed as he started to perform. Eminem was equally determined not to give up. He made it all the way through his performance, refusing to let the crowd's reaction throw him. The owner of the club was impressed by his performance and by his courage at facing the hostile crowd.

He was invited back to perform the following week. He accepted the invitation and came back that Saturday and every Saturday after that for more than a year. Gradually, he began winning the crowds over to his side. Then, he began winning competitions; soon he was winning every week. He'd succeeded in gaining respect from the very audiences that had booed his first performance.

Based on his victories, Eminem was invited to rap on WHYT, the biggest hip-hop radio station in Detroit. This was a huge break for him. Many rappers had been offered record deals based on their radio performances. Marshall was ready to take the next step in his career. But tragedy was about to occur.

TRAGEDY

On December 13, 1991, Marshall was hanging out at a friend's house when he got a frantic phone call from his mother. Ronnie Polkinghorn was dead. He had killed himself. He was only 19 years old. Marshall was devastated, finding it impossible to believe that Ronnie was dead. Not only had he lost his best friend in the world, but also, he felt responsible for his uncle's suicide.

Betty Kresin, Eminem's grandmother, told the *Village Voice* that when Debbie called Marshall with the news of Ronnie's suicide, she said, "I have some bad news for you—Ronnie's dead. And he wouldn't be if it weren't for you." According to Kresin, Debbie claimed that Ronnie had been trying to contact Marshall to talk, but that he was too busy rapping to talk to his uncle. Debbie felt that if Marshall had spoken to Ronnie, maybe he wouldn't have killed himself.

Betty Kresin said that she was with Ronnie the entire time, and that he hadn't even tried to contact Marshall. But no matter what his grandmother said to try to ease his feeling of responsibility, Marshall was filled with guilt over Ronnie's suicide. He was certain that if he had been able to speak with Ronnie, he never would have ended his own life.

Marshall was so distraught, emotionally torn apart, and guilt-ridden that he was unable to attend his beloved uncle's funeral to say good-bye.

Marshall went into a deep depression for about a year. For the first time since he was 14, he was unable to write or rap. He spent his days alone locked in his room. There, he would listen to Ronnie's rap tapes over and over. It was as if, by listening to Ronnie's voice, he was able to keep him alive.

Eventually, the depression lessened, although the pain of losing Ronnie continues. (As a tribute to his uncle, Eminem wears Ronnie's U.S. Army dog tags around his neck.) Gradually, Eminem began writing again and starting to perform locally. He was also spending a lot of time with Kim. On March 15, 1995, she informed him that he was going to be a father. On Christmas Day, December 25, 1995, his daughter, Hailie Jade, was born.

With his new family responsibilities, he started rapping with an even greater drive and energy. He was determined to make it as a rapper. He wanted only one thing—to provide for his family. He wanted to give them the things he was not able to have himself when he was growing up.

He teamed up with his friend DJ Buttafingaz. Together, they created the duo Soul Intent. They recorded an EP called *Soul Intent*. With it, Eminem began to create a buzz in Detroit's underground hip-hop scene.

Eminem came to the attention of a small company called FBT Productions. FBT, the Funky Bass Team, was a pair of Detroit hip-hop producers named Marky and Jeff Bass. They had heard Eminem rap on WHYT's late-night radio show. They were so impressed with what they heard that they offered him the chance to record his debut album.

Eminem jumped at the chance. The team advised him to concentrate on only "radio-friendly" songs. Eager to please, he wrote a series of songs about Hailie, his family, and his desire to provide for them. For example, in the song "Never Far," he says, "I got a baby on the way, I don't even got a car . . . I still stay with my moms . . . we gotta make some hit records or something [because] I'm tired of being broke . . ."

Proof, a former member of the rap group D12, was a childhood friend of Eminem. The two boys grew up together, and participated in rap battles in high school. On April 11, 2006, Proof was shot to death at a nightclub along 8 Mile Road. Eminem now has a tattoo on his lower left arm that says, "PROOF," in honor of his best friend.

The album, called *Infinite*, does not reflect the Eminem audiences now know. It lacks his trademark anger and humor. He wanted so much to be a success that he ended up compromising his artistic vision. As Eminem later said in an interview with *Rolling Stone*, "It was right before my daughter was born, so having a future for her was all I talked about. It was way hip-hopped out, like Nas or AZ—that rhyme style was real in at the time. I've always been a smartass comedian, and that's why it wasn't a good album."

The EP was released in the fall of 1996. Unfortunately for Marshall, not a single newspaper reviewed it. It received no airplay. Because of the lack of publicity, it sold very few copies. Eminem was forced to sell copies of the CD on the street out of the trunk of his car. It eventually sold approximately 500 copies.

The failure of the EP was the beginning of a downward spiral for him. Five days before Christmas 1996, he was fired from his job as a part-time chef at Gilbert's Lounge, a restaurant in St. Claire Shores. As he said in a *Rolling Stone* interview, "That was the worst time ever, dog. It was like five days before Christmas, which is Hailie's birthday. I had, like, forty dollars to get her something. I wrote [the song] 'Rock Bottom' after that."

Things only got worse. Fed up, Kim took Hailie and moved back with her parents. On top of that, she would not allow Marshall to see his daughter. He was at the end of his rope. The *Infinite* EP was a failure. He was out of a job. His girlfriend and daughter had left him. In desperation, he took an overdose of pills in an attempt at suicide. Fortunately, he survived. When he recovered he was more determined than ever to try again. He knew he was at rock bottom. There was nowhere else to go but up.

The Birth of
Slim Shady

With his old friend and mentor Proof, Eminem formed the rap troop D12. D12 is short for Detroit Twelve as well as Dirty Dozen. One of the first goals of the troop was for each member to create an alternate self, an alter ego, for himself. (There were only six members in the group. With each of them having two performing names or characters, they made up a dozen.) By having a darker half or alter ego, each member would be able to experiment with different, more hardcore styles.

Eminem was the last member of D12 to come up with a new name and character. He'd been rehired at Gilbert's Lounge (where he spent most of his time scribbling lyrics on the back of receipts). He soon got fired again and worked any job he could find to support his family. During this stressful time, he was drinking heavily. He was also getting into frequent fights.

One morning Slim Shady was born. As quoted in *Whatever You Say I Am; The Life and Times of Eminem* by Anthony Bozza, "I was sitting on the toilet and *boom* the name hit me. I started thinking of all these words I could rhyme with it."

Slim Shady liberated Marshall Mathers. With this character, he could channel his anger and rage. By exaggerating his anger and making it bigger than life, he could also make it funny. Slim Shady was the class clown who entertained everybody in school. He said things that other people thought but didn't dare say.

The things that Slim Shady said weren't always meant to be taken seriously. But then again, class clowns are willing to say or do anything to get attention. As Eminem put it, "Slim Shady is just another part of me. The dark, evil, creatively sick part."

With the birth of Slim Shady, he had found his voice. In just two weeks, he wrote the seven songs that would make the *Slim Shady EP* demo. When he arrived at the Bass Brothers studio to make the recording, he had a new $50 "Slim Shady" tattoo on his left arm. It went nicely with the "Eminem" tattoo already on his right arm.

With a new EP in hand, he was ready to conquer the world. He was mentioned in *Source* magazine's "Unsigned Hype" column. He appeared on Sway and Tech's *Wake Up Show* in Los Angeles and won their 1997 "Freestyle Performer of the Year" Award. He was getting noticed.

His personal life was still difficult. Kim and Hailie had reunited with him in Detroit, but there was never enough money, and that contributed significantly to the family's tension. He, Kim, and Hailie lived in one house after another, in progressively tougher and tougher neighborhoods. After too many robberies (they lost four televisions and five VCRs in two years) and stray bullets through their kitchen window, the struggling family moved in with Eminem's mother, Debbie.

Debbie's severe mood swings made it impossible for them to stay in her house for very long. In desperation, Kim and Hailie moved back in with Kim's parents. Marshall slept on the sofas of various friends and finally rented a room in a house with friends on 7 Mile Road.

Once again, though, disaster struck. As he recalled in *Whatever You Say I Am,* "We were paying this guy rent because his name was on the lease, but he was keeping all the money."

ALIASES AND ALTER EGOS

An alter ego is another self, a second personality. Marshall Mathers uses the stage name, or alias, Eminem. Eminem has an alter ego named Slim Shady to say the things he shouldn't. But he's not the first or last person to use an alias or alter ego.

Many other performers and writers use names other than their own, as well. For example, the writer Daniel Handler uses the alias of Lemony Snicket to write his Series of Unfortunate Events. Tupac Shakur used the alias Makaveli. Mariah Carey uses "Mimi" as her alias. Country singer Garth Brooks changed his whole look and sound to become his rock star alter ego, Chris Gaines, for the album "Garth Brooks . . . In the Life of Chris Gaines."

One of the most interesting uses of an alias or alter ego belonged to the Portuguese poet Fernando Pessoa. He wrote poetry using several different names. The poets he created included Alberto Caeiro, Alvaro de Campos, and Ricardo Reis. They all wrote in different styles and wrote about different things. Pessoa created detailed biographies for each of his alter egos. In his world, each of the poets was familiar with the work of the others, and they all commented in writing on the other writers' work! All of them existed only in the mind of Fernando Pessoa.

Everybody in the house got evicted. "The night before I went to the Rap Olympics in Los Angeles, I had to break into that house and sleep on the floor because I didn't have anywhere else to go. No heat, no electric, everything was shut off. I woke up the next day and went to L.A."

Eminem went to the competition eager to win. The Rap Olympics was a major event. Whoever won the contest would get a lot of attention and publicity. After the first round, a black audience member was heard yelling, "Just give it up to the white boy, it's all over. Just give it to the white boy."

Unfortunately for Eminem, he didn't win. As he recalled in *Whatever You Say I Am*, "I had nothing to lose. I took second place and I was very unused to that. Everyone said I looked ready to cry. And I was so mad. Steaming, dog. I had nowhere to live back home. The winner of Rap Olympics got, like, five hundred dollars. I could have used that, man. Second place got nothing."

He may have lost the competition, but his life was about to change. A copy of the *Slim Shady EP* had made it into the hands of staffers at Interscope Records. They passed it on to co-head Jimmy Iovine. Impressed, he passed it on to hip-hop legend Dr. Dre.

DR. DRE AND *THE SLIM SHADY LP*

Andre Romel "Dr. Dre" Young is one of the most important men in hip-hop. He was a member of the influential rap group N.W.A. As a solo artist he made classic albums such as *The Chronic* and *2001*. He is credited with changing hip-hop by creating West Coast G-Funk. He is also widely considered to be hip-hop's great producer. Famous for his use of synthesizers, keyboards, and heavy bass in his hip-hop beats, his services are highly in demand. Dr. Dre only works with the best. He wanted to work with Eminem.

The *Slim Shady EP* blew Dr. Dre away. He was at Jimmy Iovine's house when he heard it. As he said in *Eminem Talking*, "In my entire career in the music industry, I have never found

The great hip-hop producer and artist Dr. Dre discovered Eminem when he heard the *Slim Shady EP*. When he signed Eminem to Aftermath Entertainment, the two became fast friends and worked well together. Dr. Dre helped produce *The Slim Shady LP*, which turned out to be the breakthrough album that helped establish Eminem as a legitimate rapper.

anything from a demo tape of a CD. When Jimmy played this, I said, 'Find him. Now!'"

Eminem's passion and lyrics stood out right away for Dr. Dre, according to his quote in *Whatever You Say I Am*: "When I heard it, I didn't even know he was white. The content turned me on more than anything, and the way he was flipping it. Dark comedy is what I call it. It was incredible. I had to meet him right away."

A meeting was quickly arranged between Eminem and Dre. Eminem was nervous and starstruck. He'd been a fan of Dre's since Dre was in N.W.A. In turn, Dre couldn't believe that Eminem was a fan of his music. Before the meeting was over, Eminem had a contract with Aftermath Records (a subsidiary of Interscope Records). Dre invited Eminem to stay in Los Angeles for a week. By the end of those seven days, they had entered the studio to begin recording Eminem's new album.

Although Eminem was excited about making his first solo LP, he hadn't forgotten his friends back in Detroit. When D12 first got started, its members had made a pact: The first member of the group to achieve success as a solo artist would go back to get the others. While still in the recording studio, even before *The Slim Shady LP* had been released, Eminem proved his loyalty to his bandmates by urging Dr. Dre to sign them up as well. Dre advised him to establish himself as a solo artist first, then go back for his friends when he'd be in a better position to help them.

The two men worked together extraordinarily well. The very first day they worked together, they recorded four songs in just six hours! The rest of the recording went just as smoothly. On February 23, 1999, *The Slim Shady LP* was unleashed on the general public.

Even before the album's release, the "buzz" on it was incredible. The first single, "My Name Is…" was a big radio hit. The accompanying video was in heavy rotation on MTV. But nobody expected the CD to debut at number two on the charts. *The Slim Shady LP* sold more than 300,000 copies in just one week! It would go on to become one of the most popular albums of 1999, going triple platinum. This meant that it had sold more than 3 million copies in just the United States alone. This is a phenomenal number of CDs for a previously unknown artist.

Critics loved the album as much as the public. Looking back on the album, Stephen Thomas Erlewine of "All Music" said, "Years later, as the shock has faded, it's those lyrical skills and the subtle mastery of the music that still resonate, and they're what make *The Slim Shady LP* one of the great debuts in both hip-hop and modern pop music."

The Slim Shady LP made Eminem a star. The singles "My Name Is…" and "Guilty Conscience" were major hits. His videos were played nonstop on all the video music channels. With his all-American good looks he could have been member of a boy band. Combined with his angry and controversial lyrics, he soon was the most-talked-about new artist in America.

The album was a perfect introduction to the world of Eminem. By turns funny and serious, it presented Marshall Mathers aka Eminem aka Slim Shady in all his glory. The album sums up his life to that point. As he pointed out in *Eminem Talking*, "My album is so autobiographical that there shouldn't be any more questions to answer. It's just the story of a white kid who grew up in a black neighborhood who had a pretty [bad] life—not the worst life in the world, but still a fairly [bad] life."

The song "My Name Is…" became his first anthem, his first trademark hit. It had a bouncy beat, a catchy hook, and a nursery-rhyme-simple chorus. It quickly established the persona of Slim Shady. For Eminem, it was easy to write. As he said in *Eminem Talking*: "This was really simple to write. I thought of the hook right away, even before I wrote the song."

Other songs were less humorous, and more serious and angry. "'97 Bonnie and Clyde" imagines a trip with his daughter

Hailie. On the trip, they dispose of the dead body of Hailie's mother, Kim. How could he write a song like that? As he said in *Eminem Talking*, "That song is a joke. Kim was trying to keep me from Hailie and this was to get back at her. It's better to say it on a record than to go out and do it."

That quote described Eminem's methods in a nutshell. When he wrote the song, he was furious at Kim for keeping him away from his beloved daughter. He expressed and exaggerated his anger to the point of fantasizing murder.

Eminem got his anger out and expressed it in his music. It kept him from expressing the anger in other, perhaps more harmful, ways. Eminem said that the lyrics are not meant to be taken literally. Killing Kim may have been something that he wanted to do only in his angriest moments, but he knew he never would.

The song "Brain Damage" uses the D'Angelo Bailey incident as its basis but expands on it. By using humor and horror to exaggerate an ugly incident in his life, he was able to deal with his past. As he described the song in *Eminem Talking*,

> This is a true story except for my brain falling out of my head. I used to get harassed by these bullies in school. This one in particular, because I got a concussion, and almost died. When I wrote that, I was summing up my whole years of grade school, junior high, high school. [In the] second verse I started getting really truthful. But when I write a story, I don't want the [stuff] to get boring, so I lay down the truth as the foundation and then mix it with a little imagination.

But even this early in his career, in the song "Role Model" he made it perfectly clear that he was not a role model. The song is a list of the terrible things that he did, or that he fantasized about doing. Each verse ends with the chorus, "Don't you wanna grow up to be just like me?" To anyone who really listens to the song, it is obvious that he doesn't want his listeners to grow up like him.

Eminem's relationship with Kim Mathers is extremely tumultuous. The two met at a very young age and have had an on-again-off-again relationship since then. Eminem and Kim were first married on June 14, 1999, in St. Joseph, Missouri. The marriage didn't last long, and in 2001, Eminem and Kim got divorced.

As he said in the book *Whatever You Say I Am,*

I'm not a role model and I don't claim to be. It's what the
song "Role Model" says. I say that I do everything in the
song, but it's all . . . sarcasm. How can people not get it?
That's ridiculous. It's obviously saying, "You wanna grow
up to be just like me . . . no you don't!" The message is:
Whatever I say, do the opposite. You do that, you'll be
good, because my whole life is the opposite of good.

Eminem had a banner year in 1999. He spent two months
touring as part of the Warped Tour. He had been called in to
replace Cypress Hill, who had left the tour to begin recording their new album. The success of the tour along with the
phenomenal sales of *The Slim Shady LP* had made him rich
and famous. At last, he was able to buy Hailie all the things
he'd always wanted to.

Eminem and Kim were still having their ups and downs.
But on June 14, 1999, they got married in a nondenominational ceremony in St. Joseph, Missouri. Marshall had the
success and family he'd always wanted. Little did he know
that his newfound fame would bring with it newfound
problems.

THE PROBLEMS OF SUCCESS

One negative aspect of his success was the reaction of some
of his fellow rappers. They were amazed at Eminem's rise to
the top of the charts. His songs were getting airplay across
the United States and Europe. Even rock-and-roll stations
that had previously ignored hip-hop were playing his music.
In the ultimate act of stardom, he appeared on the cover of
Rolling Stone magazine in April 1999.

Some musicians felt that he was being embraced by the
mainstream because of his race. They claimed that black
musicians did not get half the airplay and media coverage

that Eminem did. They felt that Eminem's popularity proved that racism was still alive and well in the United States.

On some level, they were right. Eminem was getting a lot of attention because he was a white rapper, but that success is part of a long tradition. From Elvis Presley and beyond, many white performers have become popular by bringing "black" music to a white audience. Of course, the interest in hip-hop that Eminem created in the mainstream media spilled over to black hip-hop artists, as well. And Eminem is hardly responsible for the media's interest in him as a white hip-hop artist.

For Eminem, discussion of race is irrelevant. He knows that it's silly to argue whether a part of his popularity is because he is white, because he knows that it is. But he has no patience for discussions of whether he's a white guy getting rich performing black music. As he says in "The Way I Am," "And I just do not get the patience (got the patience).../To deal with these cocky Caucasians/Who think I'm some wigger who just tries to be black/'Cuz I speak with an accent."

To Eminem, hip-hop is what he is. It is so much a part of him, so much his identity as a person, that any discussion of his race is irrelevant. He's not a white artist trying to be black, and he's not pretending to be a hip-hop artist. As he said in *Eminem Talking,*

> People (who) respect the lyrics . . . can look past the whole white rapper thing. I'm not the first and I'm not gonna be the last, but hip-hop music is always gonna be predominately black. In the beginning, the majority of my shows were for all-black crowds and people would always say, "You're dope for a white boy," and I'd take it as a compliment. Then, as I got older, I started to think, "What . . . does that mean?" Nobody asks to be born; nobody has a choice of what color they'll be, or whether they'll be fat, skinny, anything. I had to work up to a certain level before people would even look past my color.

Eminem and Dr. Dre perform during the Up in Smoke Tour in 2000. Despite his legal battles, Eminem's success as an artist and performer only grew. During that same year, Eminem's *The Slim Shady LP* won two Grammy awards.

But Eminem has no patience for those who claim that hip-hop is music for blacks. He addressed the subject in *Eminem Talking*:

Whether a white kid goes through as much as I did, or didn't go through any trouble at all, if they love the music who's to tell them what they should be listening to? Let's say I'm a white 16-year old and I stand in front of the mirror and lip-synch every day like I'm Krayzie Bone—who's to say that because I'm a certain color I shouldn't be doing that? And if I've got a right to buy his music and make him rich, who's to say that I then don't have the right to rap myself?

If anything, Eminem believes that hip-hop music is a way to stop racism:

Sometimes I feel rap music is the key to stopping racism. If anything is going to at least lessen it, it's gonna be rap. I would love it if, even for one day, you could walk through a neighborhood and see an Asian guy sitting on his stoop, then you look across the street and see a black guy and a white guy sitting on their porches, and a Mexican dude walking by. If we could truly be multicultural, racism could be so past the point of anybody caring.

He had other problems to deal with besides negative backlash. In September 1999, Debbie Mathers filed a $10 million suit against him in a court of law for defamation of character. "Defamation of character" means that a person is charged with intentionally making false statements about someone. It is alleged that these statements cause harm to that person's reputation.

Debbie Mathers claimed that in various interviews and in the lyrics of his songs that Eminem had made false statements about her use of drugs and her skills as a parent. Because of the things that he'd said, she claimed that she suffered both physical and psychological injuries.

One of the lyrics specifically cited in the suit was from the song "My Name Is..." In the lyric, he says, "Ninety-nine percent of my life I was lied to/I just found out my mom does more dope than I do." Debbie denied this was true. In her suit she asked the court to award her $10 million in damages.

At one point, his mother offered to make him a deal. She would drop the defamation of character suit if he would pay her $2 million. Eminem was offended by the offer and refused. In turn, Debbie Mathers filed a second suit against her son in civil court. In this suit she claimed damages for an additional $1 million.

When Eminem responded to the suits in his deposition, he stated that the lyrics about his mother's drug use referred to her use of antidepressant drugs and tranquilizers during his childhood. He explained that his mother had been diagnosed with a number of mental health problems. Because of this, she took medication. It was these prescription drugs that he was referring to, not illegal drugs. A settlement was reached in 2001 for only $25,000. Of this, $23,000 went to her former attorney, Fred Gibson.

Eminem was furious with his mother because of her legal actions against him. As quoted in *Eminem Talking*, he said, "If my mother is cruel enough . . . knowing she didn't help me get where I'm at, try to take food out of my mouth and out of my daughter's mouth, try to take me for everything that I have, then I'm not holding back on this album [*The Marshall Mathers LP*]. She's always been out to get me, and now she knows I have money she won't leave me alone. I know that's not a nice thing to say about your mother, but unfortunately it's true."

Eminem was true to his word. He took his revenge on his mother on *The Marshall Mathers LP* with lyrics like, "my . . . mom is suing for 10 million/she must want a dollar for every pill I've been stealin/ . . . where . . . you think I picked up the habit? All I had to do was go in her room and lift up the mattress." Being Eminem has certain advantages. If someone makes him angry, it's easy to get very public revenge in his songs.

Despite the downsides of success, it brought him clout in the recording industry. Interscope Records offered him the chance to create and run his own recording label. With it, he would have total control over which groups or artists he wanted to sign and record. Eminem leapt at the opportunity. In September of 1999, he formed Shady Records. And, true to his word, the first act he signed to his new label was D12.

With just one album, Marshall Mathers had made Eminem and Slim Shady two of the most famous and controversial names in popular music. But now the pressure was on. Many artists have a successful first album but fail to reach an audience with their follow-up. It was time for Eminem to return to the studio. How would he be able to match, or even exceed, the success of *The Slim Shady LP*?

I'm Just Marshall Mathers

In early November 1999, Eminem entered the studio to begin work on his new CD. On May 23, 2000, *The Marshall Mathers LP* was released.

With it, Eminem hoped to explain himself to some of his critics. In *Eminem Talking*, he said, "This album is more serious than *Slim Shady*. It's angrier, it's not as happy-go-lucky as the last album. I just reflected on things I've been through in the last year, and wrote about it. People had some things to say about me, so I've had things to say about them."

Anyone who thought (or hoped) that the success of *The Slim Shady LP* was just a fluke would be quickly disappointed. In its first week of release, *The Marshall Mathers LP* sold nearly

2 million copies. This nearly broke *NSYNC's 2.25 million record for first week sales.

The CD debuted at number one on the charts. The same week, *The Slim Shady LP* was still holding strong at number 29 on the charts. Over the next two months, 8 million copies of *The Marshall Mathers LP* would be sold. It was obvious that Eminem was more than a flash in the pan.

Again, the critics raved. Touré wrote in *Rolling Stone*, "*The Marshall Mathers LP* is a car-crash record: loud, wild, dangerous, out of control, grotesque, unsettling. It's also impossible to pull your ears away from." Stephen Thomas Erlewine wrote in "All Music," "Eminem doesn't care if you understand exactly where he's at, and he doesn't offer any apologies if you can't sort the fact from the fiction. As an artist, he's supposed to create his own world, and with this terrific second effort, he certainly has."

The first single from the CD, "The Real Slim Shady" became a huge success. For Eminem, the song was a way of explaining that underneath the personas of Eminem and Slim Shady, he was still Marshall. As he said in *Eminem Talking*, "I'm just a regular person...Before all this rap [stuff] after all this rap [stuff] when all the fame is gone I'm going to go back to being Marshall Mathers. Nobody's going to give a [care] about me—before they didn't."

In "The Real Slim Shady," Slim blithely insults various celebrities (Christina Aguilera and Will Smith, among others). He attacks the popularity of boy bands: "I'm sick of you little girl and boy groups, all you do is annoy me/So I have been sent here to destroy you." He also attacks the hordes of newly arrived Eminem imitators. But, it was the song's bouncing rhythms and catchy sing-along chorus line, "Won't the real Slim Shady please stand up, please stand up, please stand up?" that helped make the song a worldwide hit.

Eminem accepts the Best Male Video award for his song "The Real Slim Shady" at the 2000 MTV Video Music Awards. "The Real Slim Shady" was his first single on his second album, *The Marshall Mathers LP*. The song and album were an instant success.

The accompanying video, directed by Philip Atwell and Dr. Dre, was equally successful. A hilarious look inside the head of Marshall's alter ego Slim Shady, the video aired virtually nonstop on MTV. It went on to win MTV Video Awards for Best Male Video as well as Best Video.

The next singles released from the album, "The Way I Am" and "Stan," were much more serious. "The Way I Am" explores the pressures the record company put on him to top the success

GRAMMYS

The Recording Academy presents the Grammy Awards to recognize outstanding achievements in the recording industry. Grammys are currently awarded in 108 categories within 30 different genres, or types, of music. These genres include pop, gospel, rap, country, and classical. Peers vote on the awards. Peers are other musicians who are voting members of the Academy.

As a trophy, Grammy winners receive a small gilded statuette of a gramophone. A gramophone is an early version of a record player. The award's name is a short form of the word "gramophone."

The awards were first presented in 1959. Since then, thousands of the world's greatest recording artists have received Grammy Awards. Sir George Solti, the late conductor of the Chicago Symphony Orchestra, received more Grammys than any other person. He received 31 Grammys over the course of his career.

Alison Krauss has taken home 20 Grammy Awards, more than any other female artist or any country artist. The most Grammys won in a single night is eight. Michael Jackson and Carlos Santana share that record.

of "My Name Is…." Instead of delivering the funny "commercial" song that the company wanted, he wrote "The Way I Am."

In his book *Angry Blonde*, Eminem said, "The label wanted a single, so I gave 'em "The Way I Am," which was the complete opposite of what they requested. I was kinda rebelling against the label by letting them know they couldn't force me to do something that I didn't want to do."

In the song, he talks about pressures from his label and his fans, and about being the target of the media. He talks about the eagerness of the media to blame artists like him and Marilyn Manson for events such as the killings at Columbine High School. He felt that the blame lies with the parents. The song was another huge success.

The third single, "Stan," has become a modern-day classic. In the song (which samples Dido's "Thank You") Eminem tries to cope with his fame. The song is written from the point of view of a deranged fan. The fan kills himself and his pregnant girlfriend when he gets no response to his letters to Eminem. In the final verse, too late, Eminem reaches out to the fan. He apologizes for not responding. He tries to make him understand that his lyrics are not to be taken seriously.

The album was a giant step forward for Eminem. It's darker, deeper, and even more personal than *The Slim Shady LP*. Talking about his own life, about growing up in a broken home and working dead-end jobs, and about his problems with drugs, he spoke to a greater audience than ever before. His music was played not only on Top 40 and hip-hop stations. It was played on classic rock and alternative rock stations as well. White and black, hip-hop and rock, it seemed that everybody was listening to Eminem. With additional popularity, however, came additional controversy.

LEGAL AND PERSONAL PROBLEMS

Since 1995, Eminem and the Insane Clown Posse had been involved in a feud. The ICP was a "horrorcore" rap outfit known for their evil clown makeup and hardcore lyrics. The feud started when Eminem was booked to perform at a party in Detroit. Allegedly, he passed out flyers promoting the event. The flyers stated that the ICP would also be performing there. ICP was furious, thinking that Eminem was capitalizing on their name to get an audience for his event.

ICP attacked him in several of their songs. Eminem got back at them on *The Marshall Mathers LP.* Not only did he attack them in the song "Marshall Mathers," but also he mocked them in the skit "Ken Kaniff."

Tensions between the two camps were high on the afternoon of June 3, 2000. On that day, Eminem encountered Douglas Dail, a member of the ICP's posse, outside a car audio store in Royal Oak, Michigan. Dail began arguing with Eminem almost immediately. The actual cause of the dispute is uncertain.

The two argued for several minutes. At the same time, Eminem's wife, Kim, and Dail's wife had been shouting at each other. Eminem then allegedly pulled out a 9 mm semiautomatic Smith and Weston pistol from an ankle holster. According to Dail, Eminem began to wave the pistol in Dail's face. As soon as the gun made its appearance, everybody backed down, retreating to their cars and leaving the scene.

Several hours later, Dail reported the incident to the police. Eminem was arrested and charged with brandishing a firearm and possession of a concealed weapon. The prosecutor conceded that Eminem had not pointed the gun at Dail. Instead, it was argued, he had used it in a threatening manner.

Another ugly incident occurred the very next day. For some time, Eminem's and Kim's relationship had been troubled, in part because Kim had been upset over the way Eminem had portrayed her in his songs " '97 Bonnie and Clyde" and "Kim." In both songs, Eminem presents fictional accounts of killing his wife. In " '97 Bonnie and Clyde" he drowns her and dumps her body in a lake; in "Kim" the narrator of the song stabs her

The longstanding feud between Eminem and rap duo Insane Clown Posse *(above)* came to a head on June 3, 2000, when Eminem got into a verbal fight with Douglas Dail, a member of ICP's posse. The argument escalated and Eminem allegedly pulled out a gun and threatened Dail. Eminem was arrested and charged with brandishing a firearm and possession of a concealed weapon, to which he pleaded no contest.

to death while accusing her of cheating on him. (Marshall had long accused Kim of cheating on him with other men.)

On June 4, Marshall's anger and jealousy erupted when he saw Kim kissing a man named John Guerrera. Kim claimed that nothing had happened between Guerrera and her. Still, Marshall threatened Guerrera with a 9 mm semiautomatic gun. In addition, he was accused of pistol-whipping Guerrera. (In the song "Sing for the Moment" on the CD *The Eminem Show*, Eminem says, "Guerrera, that was a *fist* that hit you!")

For the Guerrera incident, Eminem faced charges of assault with a deadly weapon and carrying a concealed weapon without a license. After posting bail of $100,000, he was released from jail.

Kim Mathers had had enough. The pressures of instant fame and constantly fighting with her husband became too much for her. The next morning, she moved out of the family house in Sterling Heights, Michigan, taking Hailie with her. The couple had had fights before, but, to their friends, this seemed like the big one.

Things went from bad to worse. On July 7, 2000, Kim Mathers attempted suicide. She had slashed her wrists a total of five times. Discovered by Eminem's half brother Nate, she was taken to Mount Clemens General Hospital suffering from serious blood loss. It took 150 stitches to seal her cuts. Eminem was dismayed by the news and visited her in the hospital several times. He seemed to have been unaware of just how unhappy and unstable she was.

Fortunately for him, the barrage of difficulties took a positive turn. There was a plea bargain in the John Guerrera case, which concluded on April 10, 2001. Eminem pleaded guilty to weapon possession. In exchange, the more serious assault charges were dropped. He received two years' probation. He was also ordered to pay $100,000 in damages at the conclusion of the case evaluation in 2002.

In the Dail case, he pleaded nolo contendere (no contest) to the charges of firearm possession and brandishing a weapon.

The longstanding feud between Eminem and rap duo Insane Clown Posse *(above)* came to a head on June 3, 2000, when Eminem got into a verbal fight with Douglas Dail, a member of ICP's posse. The argument escalated and Eminem allegedly pulled out a gun and threatened Dail. Eminem was arrested and charged with brandishing a firearm and possession of a concealed weapon, to which he pleaded no contest.

For this, he received one year of probation. It was served simultaneously with the probation for the Guerrera case.

For many performers, rapid fame can be hard to deal with. It can lead to potentially devastating temptations. As Eminem later recalled in an interview with Frank Rich (reprinted in *White Noise: The Eminem Collection*):

> Fame hit me like a . . . ton of bricks. I was just being pulled in every direction, doing everything under the sun, two shows a day, touring constantly, nonstop radio interviews, and I just got caught up in the drinking and the drugs and fighting and just wilding out and doing dumb things I shouldn't have been doing. But I came out of them and conquered it. [If I hadn't . . .] something bad could have happened to me.

When it came to his relationship with Kim, the problems seemed insurmountable. Several months after the suicide attempt, Eminem filed for divorce from Kim, who countered with a lawsuit that sought to deny him custody of their daughter. She also asked for an additional $10 million in defamation damages.

Eminem could stand anything but the thought of losing his daughter. As he said in *Eminem Talking*, "My family is all I have ever fought for and all I've ever tried to protect. The only thing I'm scared of is being taken away from my little girl."

Fortunately the lawsuit was settled. The couple agreed to joint custody of Hailie. Kim would have physical custody, and Eminem would have liberal visitation rights. By the end of the year, though, Kim and Eminem had reconciled. Divorce claims were dropped.

MORE CONTROVERSIES

Controversy continued in his professional life, as well. Beginning in October of 2000, Eminem joined Limp Bizkit as part of the Anger Management Tour. The tour was a mixture of rap and rock acts. It included such stars as DMX and Papa Roach. It was during this tour that Eminem first came onstage wearing a hockey mask and carrying a chainsaw. His performances on this tour are considered to be among the best of his career so far. Despite his personal difficulties, he was still able to bring passion and professionalism to his shows.

Problems arose, however, before an October 26 show in Toronto, Canada. A local woman known for her opposition to violence in the media tried to prevent Eminem's entry into Canada. She filed a complaint with the Toronto Police Hate Crimes Unit, claiming that the violent lyrics of Eminem's songs could be classified as "hate propaganda" under section 319 of the Canadian Criminal Code. This states that it is illegal to make statements that intentionally promote hatred against "an identifiable group."

The day before the concert, Ontario Attorney General Jim Flaherty ruled in support of the ban. He believed that Eminem was likely to perform songs that advocated or promoted violence against women. Immigration officials were instructed to stop Eminem from entering Canada.

The following day officials from the Citizenship and Immigration Authority stepped in. They decided that they had no legal authority to refuse Eminem entry into Canada. According to the Canadian Criminal Code, an "identifiable group" only refers to color, race, religion, or ethnic origin. Under Canadian law, it was not considered a crime to promote violence against women. He would be allowed to enter the country and perform.

Based on his past actions, Eminem was not likely to ignore the controversy. He opened the concert with the song "Kill You." With lyrics such as "I'ma kill you! Like a murder weapon, I'ma conceal you/In a closet with mildew, sheets, pillows and film you..." it was one of the very songs that prompted the controversy in the first place.

When Eminem was nominated for the Album of the Year Grammy Award in 2001, controversy ensued. Many people accused Eminem of being homophobic, and claimed that the Grammys should not honor him. In response to the controversy and protests, Eminem performed his hit song "Stan" with openly gay performer Elton John. In the photograph above, Eminem and Elton John embrace at the conclusion of their performance.

After this perfomance, the National Organization for Women (NOW) attacked him. The U.S. organization claimed that his lyrics helped normalize violence against women and make it acceptable. They argued that anyone who had fantasies about murdering his wife was not and should not be a role model, and should not be touted as such by the media. The Gay-Lesbian Alliance Against Defamation (GLAAD) also attacked him, claiming he displayed a negative attitude against homosexuals. Eminem argued that he was not antigay. He has said in numerous interviews that he is not homophobic. He argues that, as an artist, he has a responsibility to push the boundaries of what is acceptable in music.

Eminem defended his lyric content and creative expression in a number of ways. For one, he claimed that his lyrics were not always meant to be taken seriously. As he says in the song "Criminal," "A lot of people think/that…what I say on records/ Or what I talk about on a record that I actually do in real life/Or that I believe it/Or that if I say I wanna kill somebody, that…/I'm actually gonna do it/Or that I believe in it…" Eminem stands by his argument that his lyrics do not always mirror his life.

He also pointed out that that his albums always came with a warning label. The label stated that only people who are 18 years old and older can purchase it. In addition, Eminem had always produced "clean" versions of his songs. These versions were acceptable for anyone to listen to on radio and television.

Much of the controversy came to a head early in 2001. When the nominations for the 2001 Grammy Awards were announced, Eminem had been nominated for three awards, including the top award of them all—album of the year. GLAAD felt that the recording industry should not be supporting an artist who they thought promoted hatred of gay people. Because of this, they announced that they would be boycotting the awards.

Eminem faced the controversy head-on. He performed his hit song "Stan" on the show. Performing the song with him was openly gay rock star Elton John, who sang the Dido portion of the song. The performance was John's idea. He told CNN, "I'm a big fan of his music, and I said I'd be delighted to. I know I'm going to get a lot of flak from various people who are going to picket the show. If I thought for one moment he was [hateful] I wouldn't do it."

The two men embraced at the end of the performance. The performance itself was well received, but it did little to answer the underlying questions about Eminem's alleged homophobia. Indeed, in later interviews, Eminem said that he hadn't even been aware that Elton John was gay, but that he respected him.

D12

Eminem used his enormous popularity as a solo artist to help his friends, just as Dr. Dre had advised from the start. In 2001, Eminem appeared on the D12 album *Devil's Night*. Considering the following he had garnered, anything with his involvement was sure to be successful. Indeed, the album was certified multiplatinum. *Devil's Night* contained the single "Purple Pills," which was renamed "Purple Hills" for radio play.

By the end of 2001, Eminem was one of the most successful recording artists in the world. The *Marshall Mathers LP* had won him two Grammy Awards: Best Rap Solo Performance for "The Real Slim Shady" and Best Rap Album for *The Marshall Mathers LP*. Would it be possible for him to top himself? What could he possibly do for an encore?

The Eminem Show

Eminem's third major album, *The Eminem Show*, was released in late spring of 2002. In its first week of release, it sold 1.3 million copies in the United States alone. It went on to sell more than 7.6 million copies by the end of the year, more than any other album that year. Despite (or maybe because of) all the controversy surrounding his name, the public still wanted to hear his music.

Consider the title: *The Eminem Show*. His first album, *The Slim Shady LP*, established the shocking and offensive character of Slim Shady and made him a star. His second album, *The Marshall Mathers LP*, explored more of his past and revealed his complexity as an artist and as a man. With *The Eminem Show*, his third album, Eminem's own public persona is the theme.

The album showed a continuing development in his music. Eminem described *The Eminem Show* as being inspired by the 1970s rock he grew up listening to. Certainly, the beats on the album are not as complex as those in his previous work. The rhythms are more rock-influenced. Their relative simplicity provides a counterpoint for Eminem's verbal gymnastics.

With this album, his lyrics show an even greater intensity and complexity. They took on an even greater importance to him, as well: For the first time, the CD includes the lyrics to all the songs.

Once again, he used his lyrics to explore his own experiences as Eminem. He took on the music industry and the puzzling phenomenon of fame. He rapped about racism and his relationships with his wife, mother, and daughter, As Anthony Bozza pointed out in the book *Whatever You Say I Am: The Life and Times of Eminem*, the album united all the styles of Eminem's music, "the lunacy of Slim Shady, the intensity of Marshall Mathers, and the savvy of Eminem—often in the same song."

Some people argued that mainstream acceptance had made Eminem soft. The lyrics on *The Eminem Show* belie that criticism. In "White America" he once again analyzed race and its role in making him a star. "I could be one of your kids White America!/Little Eric looks just like this . . . /Let's do the math/If I was black I would have sold half/" In the hit single "Without Me" he discussed how much the media needed him to play the role of the bad boy, "So the FCC won't let me be/or let me be so let me see/They try to shut me down on MTV/But it feels so empty, without me." In the same song, he acknowledged how the character Slim Shady had begun to overshadow his creator, saying, "I've created a monster, cause nobody wants to see Marshall no more/They want Shady, I'm chopped liver."

"Cleaning Out My Closet" is one of his most personal and revealing songs. In this case, the phrase "Cleaning Out My Closet" is a metaphor. He is not literally cleaning out his

In 2002, Eminem released his third album, *The Eminem Show*, which featured hit songs such as "Without Me" and "Cleaning Out My Closet." In the photograph above, Eminem performs at the 2002 MTV Video Music Awards.

closet; rather the phrase refers to Eminem looking over his past, acknowledging his mistakes, and throwing away what he no longer needs: "I maybe made some mistakes but I'm only human. But I'm man enough to face them today."

In the song, he apologizes to his mother for the pain he's caused her: "I'm sorry, Mama. I never meant to hurt you. I never meant to make you cry but tonight I'm cleanin' out my closet." He also expresses his rage at his childhood, and how his mother mistreated him. He tells her that she won't see Hailie again. He vows that, when his mother dies, Hailie will not attend her funeral. He expresses his sorrow that his mother will

DETROIT MUSIC

Music has always been an important part of Detroit's cultural scene. Throughout the 1940s and 1950s, Detroit was a major center for blues and jazz. Artists such as blues guitarist John Lee Hooker, and jazz singers Dinah Washington and Betty Carter, all made vital contributions to American music.

The 1960s saw the birth of Motown Records. Founded by Berry Gordy in 1959, Motown started as a recording studio in a small house on West Grand Boulevard. The legendary company went on to record superstars like the Supremes, Martha and the Vandellas, Stevie Wonder, and the Jackson 5. The Motown Sound, which combined pop with soul, brought many black artists to the attention of mainstream audiences.

Later still, Detroit became a home to rock music and was nicknamed "Detroit Rock City." Artists such as Grand Funk Railroad, Ted Nugent, Bob Seger, the MC5, and the Stooges all came out of the Detroit rock scene.

Today, Detroit is home to many prominent musical artists. Besides Eminem, artists such as Aaliyah, Sufjan Stevens and the White Stripes are proud to call Detroit home.

not own up to her past mistakes. Finally, he says good-bye to her, with a kind of stunning finality: "Remember when Ronnie died and you said you wished it was me? Well guess what, I am dead. Dead to you as can be."

By "cleaning out his closet" in public and sharing his life with his audience, could Eminem come to peace with his past? In the song, he acknowledges how he turns his life into entertainment: "It's my life, I'd like to welcome you all to the Eminem Show," he raps. Through his fame, his life had become like a reality TV show—a show performed beyond the boundaries of the small screen, for the whole world to participate in.

MOVIE STAR

Eminem was one of the biggest recording stars in the world. He was a star on MTV. He'd won five Grammy Awards. He'd written one book, *Angry Blonde*, which told the stories behind the songs from *The Slim Shady LP* and *The Marshall Mathers LP*. It also described his passion for his music, as well as his approach to rapping. Film seemed to beckon as Eminem's last proving ground. Would he be able to impress Hollywood in the way he had taken the music industry by storm?

The movie was called *8 Mile*. It was semiautobiographical (based on Eminem's own life), even down to the title. The title refers, of course, to the road that separates urban Detroit from its suburbs. The film tells the story of a budding rapper, Jimmy "Rabbit" Smith Jr., played by Eminem. Rabbit lives with his alcoholic mother in a trailer and has a dead-end job. Rapping is his only outlet, his way to express his anger and feelings to the world. But to win a competition at a local club he has to face the best black rappers in Detroit. If it's not exactly Eminem's life, it certainly appears to be.

The movie opened in November 2002, and the reviews were excellent. It was quickly apparent that this was not just another movie made quickly to exploit the popularity of a rap star. Critics lauded the realism of the movie and were high in their praise for Eminem's performance.

After achieving success as a rap artist, Eminem tried his hand at acting. He starred in *8 Mile*, a semi-autobiographical film that garnered critical acclaim and worldwide success. Eminem proved that he was not only a talented musician but also a talented actor. In the photograph above, Eminem attends the premiere of his film *8 Mile*.

Chicago Sun-Times critic Roger Ebert said: "Eminem survived the X-ray truth-telling of the movie camera, which is so good at spotting phonies. He is on the level. Here he plays, if not himself, a version of himself, and we understand why he has been accepted as a star in a genre mostly owned by blacks."

The movie gave Eminem a great opportunity. It gave him the time and space beyond a three-minute song or video to present all aspects of himself to the public. The performance revealed the real person behind Eminem, not the cartoon version of himself that he often played in his music and videos. *8 Mile* laid bare Eminem's roots in a way that had never been done before. It showed the world where he came from, allowing audiences to understand who he was and *why* he was the way he was.

8 Mile elevated Eminem to an even greater level of stardom. Unlikely fans such as Barbara Streisand and Meredith Viera publicly announced that they, too, liked Eminem. Even Christine Aguilera, who had been ridiculed by Eminem in the song "The Real Slim Shady," voiced her support for him at the movie's premiere.

The movie was a huge success. It earned $54 million in just its first weekend, and ultimately it grossed more than $116 million in the United States alone. Worldwide, the movie grossed more than $215 million.

In November of 2002, Eminem had the number one album (*8 Mile Soundtrack*), movie (*8 Mile*), and song ("Lose Yourself"). He was the first artist in history to accomplish this feat. "Lose Yourself" went on to become the most successful single of Eminem's career. Eminem wrote the lyrics during a break from filming *8 Mile*. He wrote all three verses quickly, in one sitting. Appearing on the *8 Mile Soundtrack*, the single reached number one in many countries, including in the United Kingdom, Australia, and New Zealand. In the United States, it became his first number-one single on the Billboard Hot 100 Singles Chart.

The song "Lose Yourself" from the motion picture *8 Mile* was awarded an Academy Award for Best Song in 2003. The win marked the first time a hip-hop song was recognized by the Academy, the film industry's highest honor. Eminem did not attend the ceremony. In the photograph above, co-writer of "Lose Yourself" Luis Resto accepts the Oscar for Best Song at the 75th Annual Academy Awards.

"Lose Yourself" won the Academy Award for Best Song—the first rap song ever to achieve this honor. Eminem did not attend the award ceremony for two reasons. First, he was certain that a rap song would not have a chance at winning. Also, it is said Eminem declined the chance to perform an altered version of the song, one in which more "acceptable" lyrics might have compromised his creative expression. Luis Resto, Eminem's keyboardist and one of the song's co-writers, attended the ceremony and accepted the award instead.

At the 2004 Grammy Awards, "Lose Yourself" earned Eminem a second nomination for Song of the Year; the first was "Without Me." Although "Lose Yourself" became the first rap song to be nominated for Song of the Year, it did not win that category. The song garnered awards for Best Male Rap Solo Performance and Best Rap Song.

Following the release and publicity drive for *8 Mile*, Eminem withdrew as much as possible from the public eye. He and Kim had finally divorced in October of 2001. Additional difficulties erupted in 2003, when Kim Mathers was charged with cocaine possession and failure to yield to an emergency vehicle. After additional charges and several missed court dates, she was sentenced to two years of probation in January of 2004.

Eminem became a full-time parent to his beloved daughter Hailie, as Kim Mathers's drug problems resulted in her loss of custody of the child. Eminem needed time to withdraw, to spend time with Hailie, and to recharge. He would not release a new album until 2004.

Just Lose It

During the period after *8 Mile*, Eminem was busy producing albums by other artists for his label, Shady Records. This included albums for D12, Obie Trice, and perhaps most important, the debut album by his protégé, 50 Cent. The album, *Get Rich Or Die Tryin'*, sold more than 6 million copies and made 50 Cent 2003's biggest new hip-hop star.

Eminem's fourth album, *Encore*, was released in November of 2004. It quickly climbed to the top of the charts, but sales were disappointing. To date, it has sold 11 million copies worldwide, compared to 19 million copies of *The Eminem Show* and 21 million copies of *The Marshall Mathers LP*.

To make matters worse, critical response to *Encore* was dismal. Many critics felt that the lyrics and production did not

After working on *8 Mile*, Eminem took a break from creating his own music, and spent his time producing albums for upcoming artists, including his protégé, 50 Cent *(above)*. Eminem signed 50 Cent to his Shady/Aftermath label, and helped produce the artist's *Get Rich or Die Tryin'* album, which became one of the biggest successes of 2003.

compare favorably with his previous albums, and that *Encore* lacked the skill and style his many fans had come to expect from Eminem. The "All Music" review charged, "[*Encore*] sounds as if Eminem is coasting, resting on his laurels, never pushing himself into interesting territory . . . *Encore* never resonates like his first three endlessly fascinating albums do."

An album by Eminem could still be counted on to draw controversy, though; it arose with the release of the album's first single, "Just Lose It," and its accompanying video. The video featured many short scenes in which Eminem lampoons himself and others. On October 12, 2004, Michael Jackson called the Los Angeles–based Steve Harvey radio show to express his unhappiness with the video. He complained that it made fun of Jackson's child molestation trial, his plastic surgeries, and an incident in which Jackson's hair caught fire during the filming of a Pepsi commercial back in 1984.

Many of Jackson's supporters in the black community decried the video. Stevie Wonder called the video "kicking a man while he's down." Steve Harvey said "Eminem has lost his ghetto pass. We want the pass back." BET (Black Entertainment Television) pulled the video from the air. MTV continued to run it, and it quickly became the #1 requested video on TRL. The controversy soon died down. To many people, the song wasn't worth protesting in the first place. They felt that the song was a weak parody, not worthy of Eminem.

More controversy erupted with the release of the single and video for "Mosh." In this song, Eminem attacks President George W. Bush with lyrics such as "this weapon of mass destruction that we call our president." The video showed Eminem leading an army of victims of the Bush administration to the White House. They break in and it is revealed that they want to register to vote. After Bush won the election, the video was changed. It showed Eminem and the protestors invading while Bush was giving a speech. "Mosh" was

In 2005, Eminem embarked on the Anger Management 3 tour, which featured artists such as 50 Cent, D12, Obie Trice, and others. Before the European leg of the tour was about to begin, Eminem pulled out due to exhaustion. Days later, he entered a rehab facility for his dependence on sleep medication.

Eminem poses for a photograph with his protégé 50 Cent *(center)* and his mentor, Dr. Dre. When he's not working on his own music, Eminem collaborates with other artists and helps produce records for upcoming rappers. Although the media constantly speculates about his career, Eminem keeps his life and work private.

the most overtly political song that Eminem had written to date.

In the summer of 2005, Eminem began his first U.S. concert tour in three years. It was called the Anger Management 3 Tour. It featured performers such as Lil Jon, 50 Cent and G-Unit, D12, Obie Trice, the Alchemist, and others.

In August of 2005 he canceled the European leg of his tour, citing exhaustion. Several days after canceling the tour, it was announced that Eminem had checked himself into a hospital in Michigan to receive treatment for his dependence on sleep medications.

There were other problems as well. His aunt and uncle, Jack and Betty Schmitt, had sued him. They claimed that he had gone back on a promise to build a $350,000 house for them.

They said that Eminem had also promised to provide them with money for the house's upkeep. The couple claimed that Eminem had kept the house in his name and then served them with eviction papers.

On top of everything else, rumors swirled that Eminem was on the verge of retirement. Some people thought that *Encore* had reflected Eminem's ambivalence about which area of his creative life to concentrate on. The *Detroit Free Press* claimed that members of his inner circle said that he wanted to retire from performing and concentrate on producing. These same people supposedly claimed that he wanted to spend more time with his daughter and niece. It was also reported that he wanted to do more movies.

Eminem denied the rumors. He told MTV News, "When I say I'm taking a break, I'm taking a break from my music to go in the studio and produce my other artists and put their albums out. When I know my next move, I'll tell everyone my next move."

That's all his fans wanted to know. What would Eminem do next?

The End of
Slim Shady?

Eminem's next album was called *Curtain Call: The Hits.* The title did little to dispel the rumors of his retirement. After all, a curtain call occurs at the end of a performance, when the performer comes on stage for one last bow. Was Eminem saying that this was his final bow?

Eminem neither confirmed nor denied the rumors of his retirement. In an interview on the release date of the CD, on WKQI's Mojo in the Mornin' radio show, he said: "I'm at a point in my life right now where I feel like I don't know where my career is going . . . This is the reason that we called it *Curtain Call,* because this could be the final thing. We don't know."

The CD was a greatest hits compilation with three new songs. One of the new songs, "When I'm Gone" seems to offer

On January 14, 2006, Eminem and Kim married for the second time. Their attempt at reconciliation was short-lived. Eminem filed for divorce just weeks later. In the photograph above, a limousine arrives at Oakland University's Meadowbrook Hall, where the two were married.

a few clues to Eminem's future. The song is about the effect that Eminem's career has had on his wife and daughter. In a "dream" his daughter Hailie confronts him at a concert in Sweden. She wants to know why he has been so cruel toward Kim. She goes on to tell him that he loves his fame, career, and fans more than his own family.

After she leaves, Eminem turns around and sees a gun. He picks it up and screams, "Find a gun on the ground/cock it, put it to my brain/scream 'Die Shady!' and pop it." After that

Eminem and his brood live in Clinton Charter Township, just outside of Detroit. The photograph above is an exterior shot of what is believed to be Eminem's house.

he wakes up, realizing that it was only a dream. Outside it is spring. Hailie is outside playing. He kisses Kim.

The song illustrates the difficulties that Eminem has had coping with fame. It also shows the difficulty of coping with his alter ego, Slim Shady. Where does Marshall Mathers end, and where does Shady begin? In the song, he seems to be willing to kill off Slim Shady if it will bring happiness to his family.

REMARRIAGE

Eminem still refused to give up on his dream of having a happy and united family. On January 14, 2006, he married Kim a second time. She was the love of his life and he was willing to give it another chance, both for Kim's sake as well as Hailie's.

After selling millions of albums, and receiving numerous awards, Eminem has proven himself as one of the greatest rappers of his time. He has brought rap music to a larger audience and has defied racial stereotypes associated with hip-hop.

Unfortunately, the attempt at remarriage was a failure. Fewer than 11 weeks after remarrying Kim, Eminem filed for divorce. Court papers cited "a breakdown in the marriage relationship." Since the divorce was finalized on December 21, 2006, the couple has shared custody of Hailie.

Eminem's home for Hailie is in Clinton Charter Township, Michigan, on the outskirts of Detroit. He also cares for Kim's niece Alaina, whom Kim and Eminem adopted. Taking care of the children in his life seems to be Eminem's top priority. As he said in an interview in the November 24, 2004, issue of *Rolling Stone*, "I just want my immediate family . . . to have things I didn't have: love and material things. But I can't just buy them things. I have to be there."

What seems to matter to Marshall Mathers is finding a balance. Eminem needs music as an outlet. Marshall needs to be with his kids. And Slim Shady? He may have served his purpose, and might be gone forever.

Whether Eminem will make another record is anyone's guess. But he definitely will continue to be an important part of the music scene by producing other people's records. He has announced that he's going to star in a new movie. It's going to be a big-screen adaptation of the 1950s Western television series *Have Gun Will Travel*. In it, Eminem will play gun-for-hire Paladin. It is planned that the story will be set in the present day, possibly in Detroit. Eminem will be involved with the soundtrack.

Even if Eminem never makes another album, his place in music history is secure. His first three albums, *The Slim Shady LP, The Marshall Mathers LP,* and *The Eminem Show* are acknowledged masterpieces of hip-hop. By using alter egos to escape the troubles of his childhood, he created music that has inspired, challenged, and defined a generation. If he does decide to make another album, the world will be eager to hear what he has to say.

DISCOGRAPHY

Infinite (1996)
The Slim Shady EP (1997)
The Slim Shady LP (1999)
The Marshall Mathers LP (2000)
The Eminem Show (2002)
8 Mile Soundtrack (2002)
Encore (2004)
Curtain Call: The Hits (2005)

FILMOGRAPHY

Da Hip-Hop Witch (2000) (Appearance)
The Wash (2001) (Cameo)
8 Mile (2002) (Starring)

▶ ▶▶ CHRONOLOGY ▪ ‖

1972   **October 17** Marshall Bruce Mathers III, known as Eminem, is born in St. Joseph, Missouri, to Deborah "Debbie" Mathers-Briggs and Marshall Mathers Jr.

1973-1987 Marshall Mathers Jr. abandons his family. Eminem and his mother move back and forth between Missouri and Michigan, finally settling in Detroit, Michigan.

1989 Eminem drops out of high school to focus on his hip-hop career.

1991 **December 13** Eminem's Uncle Ronnie kills himself, sending Eminem into a year-long depression.

1995 **December 25** Daughter Hailie is born to longtime girlfriend Kimberly Ann "Kim" Scott.

1996 Eminem records his first EP, *Infinite.* It is not a success, and Eminem attempts suicide.

1997 He develops the character of Slim Shady and records *The Slim Shady EP.*

He comes to the attention of Dr. Dre. and signs with Interscope Records.

1999 Release of *The Slim Shady LP.*

2000 Release of *The Marshall Mathers LP.*

Eminem is arrested in separate incidents with John Guerrera and the rap group Insane Clown Posse. He avoids jail and receives probation for both cases.

Wins two Grammy Awards for best rap solo performance and best rap album.

2001 Eminem and Kim divorce, sharing custody of Hailie.

2002 Release of the CD *The Eminem Show.*

Eminem stars in the semi-autobiographical film *8 Mile.*

2003 Eminem receives an Academy Award for Best Song for "Lose Yourself."

2004 Release of the CD *Encore*.

2005 Release of the CD *Curtain Call: The Hits*.
Rumors swirl that he will retire from recording.

2006 **January 14** Eminem remarries Kim.

December 5 Eminem releases the CD compilation *Eminem Presents the Re-Up*, featuring artists from the Shady Records roster.

TIMELINE

1972
Marshall Bruce Mathers III is born in St. Joseph, Missouri.

1996
Eminem records his first EP, *Infinite*. It is not a sucess, and Eminem attempts suicide.

1999
Release of *The Slim Shady LP*.

1972

2000

1995
Daughter Hailie is born to longtime girlfriend Kimberly Ann "Kim" Scott.

1997
The Slim Shady EP comes to the attention of Dr. Dre and Interscope Records.

2000
The release of The Marshall Mathers LP.

December 21 Eminem and Kim's second divorce is finalized. The couple agrees to split their property and share custody of Hailie.

2007   **February 16** The war of words between Eminem and Kim continues as Kim blasts her former husband in a radio interview. Eminem responds, "I've moved on and she hasn't. . . for the sake [of the children] I wish she would stop."

Eminem's second movie, *Have Gun Will Travel*, begins production, with a 2008 release date planned.

2001
Eminem and Kim divorce, sharing custody of Hailie.

2003
Receives an Academy Award for Best Song for "Lose Yourself."

2007
Eminem's second movie, *Have Gun Will Travel*, begins production.

2001   2007

2002
Release of the CD *The Eminem Show*. Eminem stars in the semi-autobiographical film *8 Mile*.

January 14, 2006
Eminem remarries Kim.

December 21, 2006
Eminem's and Kim's second divorce is finalized.

GLOSSARY

bling   Expensive jewelry.

break dancing   A dynamic, acrobatic style of dance.

conspicuous consumption   The purchase or display of material goods with the intention of impressing others

defamation   An accusation or attack on a person's character or name.

EP   A record longer than a single but shorter than a full album.

gangsta rap   Subculture of rap music focusing on street violence and gangsters.

griot   Musician-entertainers of western Africa who recite tribal histories and genealogies.

homophobia   Fear of and discrimination against homosexuals.

horrorcore   Genre of hip-hop that blends hardcore rap with elements of horror films.

LP   Phonograph record album.

MCs   Short for "microphone coordinator," the MC vocalizes rhymes to acknowledge the deejay and stir excitement in the crowd.

misogyny   Hatred of women.

nondenominational   Not restricted to a particular religious denomination

posse   A group.

remixes   Alternate mixes or arrangements of songs, usually for dance purposes.

sample   An excerpt from a musical recording used in another recording.

scratching   A deejay technique that results from the manual manipulation of a turntable to create a variety of sounds.

BIBLIOGRAPHY

Als, Hilton, and Darryl Turner, eds. *White Noise*. New York: Thunder Mouth Press, 2003.

Bozza, Anthony. "Eminem Blows Up." *Rolling Stone* 811 (1999): 42–47.

———. *Whatever You Say I Am: The Life and Times of Eminem*. New York: Crown Publisher, 2003.

Christgau, Robert, "White American: Eminem Makes His Rock Move," robertchristgau.com. Available online. URL: www.robertchristgau.com/xg/rock/eminem-02.php.

Ebert, Roger, "8 Mile," rogerebert.com. Available online. URL: http://rogerebert.com.suntimes.com/apps/pbcs.dll/article?AID=20021108/REVIEWS/21108031/1023.

Eddy, Chuck. "The Daddy Shady Show." *The Village Voice* (December 25–31, 2002).

Eminem, *Angry Blonde*. New York: ReganBooks, 2002.

Erlewine, Stephen Thomas. "The Slim Shady LP," All Music. Available online. www.allmusic.com.

———. "The Marshall Mathers LP," All Music. Available online. URL: www.allmusic.com.

———. "The Eminem Show," All Music. Available online. URL: www.allmusic.com.

———. "Encore," All Music. Available online. URL: www.allmusic.com.

Gigney, Scott, and Martin Harper. *His Name Is: The Eminem Story in Words and Pictures*. Chicago, Ill.: Independent Publishers Group, 2001.

"Shady's Big-Screen Return," *Rolling Stone* (July 13–27, 2006).

Touré, "The Marshall Mathers LP," *Rolling Stone*. Available online. URL: http://www.rollingstone.com/reviews/album/315749/the_marshall_mathers_lp.

———. "The Serious Side of Eminem," *Rolling Stone.* Available online. URL: www.rollingstone.com/news/coverstory/serious_side_of_eminem.

Weiner, Chuck. *Eminem Talking.* London, UK: Omnibus Press, 2002.

Wikipedia. "Breakdance." Available online. URL: http://en.wikipedida.org/wiki/Breakdance.

———. "Detroit, Michigan." Available online. URL: http://en.wikipedia.org/wiki/Detroit.

———. "Elvis Presley." Available online. URL: http://en.wikipedia.org/wiki/Elvis_Presley.

———. "Eminem." Available online. URL: http://en.wikipedia.org/wiki/Eminem.

———. "The Eminem Show." Available online. URL: http://en.wikipedia.org/The_Eminem_Show.

———. "History of Hip-Hop Music." Available online. URL: http://en.wikipedia.org/History_of_hip_hop_music.

▸ ▸ FURTHER READING ■ ‖

BOOKS

Ayazi-Hashijn, Sherry. *Rap & Hip-Hop: The Voice of a Generation.* New York: Rosen Publishing Group, 1999.

Baker, Soran. *The Music Library—The History of Rap and Hip-Hop.* San Diego, Calif.: Lucent Books, 2006.

Gay, Cheri Y. *Detroit Then & Now.* San Diego, Calif.: Thunder Bay Press, 2001.

Hoffman, Frank, ed. *American Popular Music: Rhythm & Blues, Rap, and Hip-Hop.* New York: Facts on File, 2005.

Lane, Stephanie. *Eminem* (People in the News). San Diego, Calif: Lucent Books, 2005.

Lommell, Cookie. *The History of Rap Music.* New York: Chelsea House, 2001.

WEB SITES

www.azlyrics.com/e/eminem/html

www.eminem.com

www.eminem.net

www.shadybase.com

www.vh1.com/artists/az/artist.jhtml

www.rollingstone.com/artists/eminem

▸▸ PHOTO CREDITS ▪▮

▸ ▸ INDEX ▪ ▐▐

50 Cent, 79–80, 83
8 Mile, 74–78
8 Mile Road, 23–24
"'97 Bonnie and Clyde", 19,
  47–48, 61–63

A
abuse, 21–22. *See also* drug
  abuse
Academy Awards, 77–78
acting, 74–78, 89
"Adventures on the Wheels of
  Steel" (Grandmaster Flash),
  29
Afrika Bambaataa, 6–7
Aftermath Records, 46
Aguilera, Christina, 57, 76
alcohol, 42
aliases, defined, 43
alter egos, defined, 43
anger, 19, 21, 48, 73–74
Anger Management 3 Tour, 82,
  83
Anger Management Tour, 66
Angry Blonde, 74
arrests, 61, 62, 63–64
Atwell, Philip, 59
Australia, 8
automobile industry, 25
awards
  Academy, 77–78
  "Freestyle Performer of the
    Year", 42
  Grammy, 13, 52, 59, 67–69
  MTV Best Male Video, 58
  multiple, 12

B
Bailey, D'Angelo, 26–27, 48
Bambaataa, Africa, as founding
  father, 6–7
Bass Brothers studio, 42

battle rapping, 33, 39
Beastie Boys, influence of, 33,
  34
birth name, 11, 26
birthday, 26
blood poisoning, 20
Blow, Kurtis, 29, 30
"Bonnie and Clyde", 19, 47–48,
  61–63
Boogaloo Shrimp, 31
"Brain Damage", 27, 48
Brazil, 9
break dancing, 29, 32
Breakin', 29, 31
bullies, 24–27
Bush, George W., 81
Buttafingaz, 38

C
Caeiro, Alberto, 43
Campos, Alvaro de, 43
Canada, 66
Chateau Clinton, 26
civil rights, music and, 8
"Cleaning Out My Closet",
  21–22, 71–74
Clinton Carter Township, MI,
  87, 88
coma, 27
Comerica Park, 25
controversy, 17–19, 60–61,
  65–69, 81
"Criminal", 68
Curtain Call: The Hits, 85–86
Cypress Hill, 49

D
D12, 41, 46, 55, 69, 79
Daddy Warbucks, 20
Dail, Douglas, 61, 62
defamation of character law-
  suits, 52–53, 65

Detroit, 23–27, 31–32, 73
Detroit River Walk, 25
Devil's Night (D12), 69
DJ Buttafingaz, 38
Dr. Dre, 44–46, 52
Dr. D, 59, 83
drug abuse
    Debbie Mathers and, 22–23
    Detroit and, 24, 25
    Kim Mathers and, 78
    lawsuits and, 53–54
    sleep medication and, 82, 83
    temptations of fame and, 65

E
Ebert, Roger, 76
8 Mile, 74–78
8 Mile Road, 23–24
emcees, roots of hip-hop and, 29
The Eminem Show, 15, 21–22, 70–74
Encore, 21, 79–82
Erlewine, Stephen, 47, 57
"Evil Deeds", 21

F
Fatback Band, 29
50 Cent, 79–80, 83
Flaherty, Jim, 66
founding fathers, 6–7
France, 8
"Freestyle Performer of the Year" award, 42
Funky Bass Team (FBT) Productions, 38
Funky Bunch, 35

G
Gaines, Chris, 43
gangsta rap, 15
Gay-Lesbian Alliance Against Defamation (GLAAD), 68

Get Rich or Die Tryin', 79–80
Gibson, Fred, 54
Gilberts Lounge, 40, 41
Gordy, Berry, 73
Graceland, 16
Grammy awards, 13, 52, 59, 67–69
Grandmaster Flash, 6–7, 28
Grandwizard Theodore, 29
griots, defined, 28
Guerrera, John, 63
"Guilty Conscience", 47

H
hate propaganda, 66
hatred, controversy over, 17
Have Gun Will Travel, 89
"Heartbreak Hotel" (Presley), 13
hip hop music, roots of, 28–29
Hip-Hop-Club, 36
homophobia, 17, 67, 68–69

I
Ice-T, 31
Infinite, 40
Insane Clown Posse (ICP), feud with, 60–62
Interscope Records, 44, 46, 55
Iovine, Jimmy, 44

J
Jackson, Michael, 59, 81
Japan, 8
John, Elton, 67, 68–69
"Just Lose It", 81

K
"Ken Kaniff", 61
"Kill You", 66
"Kim", 19, 61–63
"King Tim III (Personality Jock)" (Fatback Band), 29

Kool DJ Herc, 6–7, 28
Krauss, Alison, 59
Kresin, Betty (grandmother), 37

L
lawsuits
Debbie Mathers and, 52–53
Jack and Betty Schmitt and, 83–84
Kim Mathers and, 65
Lemony Snicket, 43
Limp Bizkit, 65–66
"Lose Yourself", 76–78
Loyal to the Game (Tupac Shakur), 11

M
Makaveli, 43
Marky Mark, 35
"Marshall Mathers", 61
The Marshall Mathers LP, 54–55, 56–60, 69, 74
Mathers, Alaina (adopted daughter), 88
Mathers, Debbie (mother)
"Cleaning Out My Closet" and, 72–74
death of Ronnie and, 37
defamation of character lawsuit of, 52–53
early life with, 20–23, 26
moving in with, 42–43
revenge on through lyrics, 54–55
Mathers, Hailie Jade (daughter), 38, 78, 88
Mathers, Kim (wife)
"'97 Bonnie and Clyde" and, 48
birth of Hailie and, 38
divorce from, 78
estrangement from, 40
filing for divorce from, 65

initial meeting with, 35
marriage to, 49, 50, 86, 87–88
portrayal of in songs, 61–63
writing about, 17
Mathers, Marshall Bruce III, as birth name, 11, 26
Mathers, Marshall Jr. (father), 20–21
MC Proof, 33, 39, 41
MCs, 29
misogyny, 17, 68
"Mosh", 81–83
Motown Records, 73
movies, 74–78, 89
MTV Best Male Video award, 58
Munchausen by proxy, 21–22
"My Name Is...", 19, 46–47, 53

N
National Organization for Women (NOW), 68
Nelson, Debbie (mother). *See* Mathers, Debbie (mother)
"Never Far", 38
"'97 Bonnie and Clyde", 19, 47–48, 61–63
Notorious B.I.G., death of, 15
N.W.A., 44, 46

O
Obie Trice, 79
Olympics, Rap, 44
Osborn High School, 33

P
percussion breaks, extended, 28
Pessoa, Fernando, 43
pistol-whipping, 63
Polkinghorn, Ronnie (nephew/ uncle), 23, 27, 31, 36, 37–38
poverty, 21
Presley, Elvis, influence of, 13–

15, 16, 51
probation, 63, 64
Proof, 33, 39, 41
"Purple Pills" (D12), 69

R
"Rabbit", 74–78
race riots, 25
Radiotron, 29
rap music, defined, 7
Rap Olympics, 44
"Rappers Delight" (Sugarhill
   Gang), 7, 29
"The Real Slim Shady", 57, 58
rehab, 82, 83
Reis, Ricardo, 43
Resto, Luis, 76–78
retirement rumors, 84, 85–86
riots, race and, 25
"Rock Bottom", 40
"Role Model", 48–50

S
sales, statistics on, 11, 57, 70, 76,
   79
Samra-Mathers, Nathan (half-
   brother), 21, 31, 63
Santana, Carlos, 59
Schmitt, Jack and Betty (aunt
   and uncle), 83–84
schools, 26–27, 35
Scott, Kimberly Ann (wife). See
   Mathers, Kim (wife)
Shady Records, 55, 79
Shakur, Tupac, 11, 15, 43
Shrimp, Boogaloo, 31
"Sing for the Moment", 63
Slim Shady, 11, 17–19, 41–44. See
   also "The Real Slim Shady"
Slim Shady EP, 42, 44–50
The Slim Shady LP, 27, 45–50, 74

Smith, Will, 57
snowball incident, 26–27
Solti, George, 59
Soul Intent, 38
sound tracks, 76–77
stage name, origins of, 34
"Stan", 59–60, 67, 68–69
subject matter, 15–17
success, 50–55, 59–60, 65
Sugarhill Gang, 7, 29
suicide, 37, 40, 63

T
temptations, 65
Toronto, Canada, 66
toxemia, 20
Tupac Shakur, 11, 15, 43

U
Up in Smoke Tour, 52

V
Vanilla Ice, 17, 35

W
warning labels, 68
Warped Tour, 49
"The Way I Am", 51, 59–60
weapons, 61, 62, 63–64
West Africa, roots of hip-hop
   and, 28–29
West Coast G-Funk, 44
"When I'm Gone", 85–86
"White America", 71
WHYT, 37
"Without Me", 14, 15, 71, 78
women, 17, 68
Wonder, Stevie, 81

Y
Young, Andre Romel, 44–46, 52

► ►► ABOUT THE AUTHORS ■ ❚❚

DENNIS ABRAMS is the author of several books for Chelsea House, including biographies of Barbara Park, Anthony Horowitz, Hamid Karzai, and Ty Cobb. He attended Antioch College, where he majored in English and communications. A voracious reader since the age of three, Dennis currently lives in Houston with his partner of 18 years.

CHUCK D redefined rap music and hip-hop culture as leader and co-founder of legendary rap group Public Enemy. His messages addressed weighty issues about race, rage and inequality with a jolting combination of intelligence and eloquence. A musician, writer, radio host, television guest, college lecturer, and activist, he is the creator of Rapstation.com, a multi-format home on the web for the vast global hip-hop community.